IN THE

ENEMY'S CAMP

IN THE ENEMY'S CAMP

Suzanne Sparrow Watson
with
Kathleen Chapman Watson

iUniverse, Inc.
New York Lincoln Shanghai

IN THE ENEMY'S CAMP

All Rights Reserved © 2004 by Suzanne Sparrow Watson

No part of this book may be reproduced or transmitted in any form or by any means, graphic, electronic, or mechanical, including photocopying, recording, taping, or by any information storage retrieval system, without the written permission of the publisher.

iUniverse, Inc.

For information address:
iUniverse, Inc.
2021 Pine Lake Road, Suite 100
Lincoln, NE 68512
www.iuniverse.com

ISBN: 0-595-30877-5

Printed in the United States of America

Contents

Map of the Philippine Islands vii
Chapman/Watson Family—1942 ix
First Date xiii
A Long Look Back xv
CHAPTER 1   The Glorious East 1
CHAPTER 2   Protective Custody 16
CHAPTER 3   The Diary 38
CHAPTER 4   Hope and Hunger 62
CHAPTER 5   The Beginning of the End 77
CHAPTER 6   The American Dream 89
Epilogue 97
Afterword 101
Author's Note 105
Bibliography 107

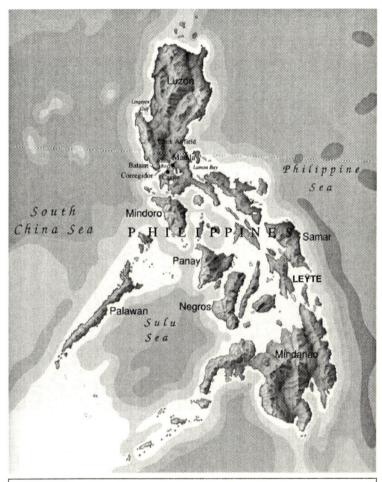

Philippine map courtesy of the General Libraries,
The University of Texas at Austin.

CHAPMAN/WATSON FAMILY - 1942

Thomas Chapman – b. 1873
m.
Dora Talbot Chapman – b.1888

Doreen Chapman – b. 1910

Tommy Chapman – b. 1912
m.
Lolita Luling

Carol – b. 1938

Kathleen Chapman Watson - b. 1914
m.
Daniel Jackson Watson – b. 1907

Richard – b. 1937
Alan – b. 1941

Jack Chapman – b. 1921

Acknowledgements

I am grateful to the many people who helped me through the process of writing this remarkable story. First and foremost, my thanks go to Robert and Rosemary Turner, David Bragg, Donna Boss and Bob Sparrow for reading through the early drafts of the manuscript and offering me sage advice.

I am also in debt to the veterans who responded to my request in *The Saber,* the First Cavalry newsletter, seeking surviving members of the team that liberated Santo Tomas. They were: Claude Walker, Jr., Chelly Mendoza, Jack Pike, John Yunker and Bob Holland. Proving that it is indeed a small world, Bob had recently completed a book about the rescue of Santo Tomas (see bibliography) and we discovered that he lives only 10 miles from us. He is truly a gentle man and now a friend forever. I was extremely touched by all of these veterans and their willingness to share their stories. Their rescue of my husband and his family made possible the life I lead today. I cannot thank them enough.

I am indebted to my husband for encouraging me to complete my dream of writing a book. Our children, Colin, Wendy and Steve, also cheered me on during this process and it is for them, as well as for our grandsons, Matthew and Jake, that this book is written.

And, finally, my deep gratitude goes to Kathleen Watson. Not only did she write the diary that is the basis for this book, she provided me with untold stories and photographs from her personal collection. She is an inspiration not only because of her prison camp experience, but for the way she chooses to live her life every day. She is indeed one of a kind.

Suzanne Watson
Scottsdale, Arizona
December, 2003

First Date

Up to a point, it was a typical first date. My future husband, Alan, took me to one of the best restaurants in San Francisco, complete with red leather banquettes and pretentious waiters. We sipped our first cocktail and began the conversational volleyball that attends all such dates, discussing politics and sports teams, while searching for some area of common interest. Towards the end of dinner, Alan set up the conversation that consumed the rest of our evening: he asked me what my ethnic heritage was. I thought it was an odd question, but answered that I was a mix of several northern European nationalities. I expected to hear something similar from him, given his blond hair and blue eyes. I could not have been more surprised when he leaned across the table and said, "I'm a Filipino."

I listened intently for the next hour to his compelling tale of adventure, romance, imprisonment and achievement. His story centered on the revelation that he and his family had been interned in a Japanese prisoner of war camp in Manila during World War II. When the Japanese Army occupied Manila at the beginning of 1942 they had captured Alan's parents, brother, grandparents, aunts, uncles and cousin. The story of why his family had been living in the Philippines was as fascinating as their war-time experience.

Alan mentioned off-handedly that his mother kept a diary during their internment. She started the diary in 1944, several months after her parents left Manila for the United States as part of a civilian prisoner exchange. She hoped it would ease her feelings of loneliness for her repatriated parents and document for them the horrendous conditions under which she was living. Alan told me that he had not read the diary in many years, but recalled that the diary's style was a bit quirky; instead of the conventional format, his mother had written each entry as if it was a letter to her parents.

Alan and I eventually married and I was fortunate to hear the family story firsthand from his parents. In 1987, his mother, Kathleen, gave her children and grandchildren a typewritten history of the family that included her war-time chronicles. The diary contained a compelling account of her prison camp experience that I have re-read many times over the ensuing years.

I later learned that my in-laws were among more than 7,000 Allied civilians, mostly Americans, who were interned by the Japanese throughout the Philippine

Islands during World War II. On January 1, 1942, the Japanese occupying forces marched into metropolitan Manila searching for Allied citizens residing in the city. Four days later, they rounded up 300 American and British civilians and placed them into the classroom and administrative buildings of Santo Tomas University. By the end of January, the University had become the largest internment camp in the Philippines, with a population of more than 3,600 prisoners.

Most of the prisoners were American businessmen and their families, sent to the Philippines to take part in the commercial development of Manila that had begun forty years earlier. The internees began a three year journey that January that tested their mental and physical fortitude. Many wouldn't make it. Those that did reached the limits of will and determination.

In 2003 I suggested to Kathleen that we publish a book detailing her experiences so others might read about this little-known aspect of the war. Fortunately, she agreed to share her story. This book is not intended to be *the* definitive story of the Santo Tomas Internment Camp. Every person experienced the camp from a different perspective: some were married with children, while others were single and just starting out in life; some had the money to buy additional food, while their neighbors were forced to subsist of the meager provisions provided in the camp.

This book chronicles one story of the 3,600 brave citizens who endured and survived Santo Tomas.

A Long Look Back

Kathleen Watson sat in the comfort of her Pasadena home looking out the window at the pouring rain. The sky had taken on the dull grey color that forms when the clouds and rain chase away the pervasive smog. It had been raining continuously for two days and the news reports on television were full of stories about flooded streets and stranded motorists. Kathleen was bemused by the news anchors, whose warnings about rain damage and the possible after-effects of the storm seemed overly dramatic. "If only they had been in Santo Tomas," she muttered in disgust. As she continued to watch the rain fall, her thoughts turned to Manila, and the ghastly three years she had spent in Santo Tomas internment camp. She had endured bad conditions on most days, but when it rained those conditions became intolerable. "Stranded motorists, indeed," she thought, "they should experience a monsoon where there are no paved roads or sufficient shelter."

Kathleen looked out on the *pomolo* tree that stood on the far side of the patio. She had brought the *pomolo* seed into the United States after one of her return visits to the Philippines. She marveled at how the tree had flourished in the Southern California sunshine; it now stood almost twenty feet high. The rain pooled on its broad, glossy leaves and fell to the ground forming small pools on the concrete below. She gazed at the tree, her thoughts returning to Santo Tomas and another rainy day when she was just twenty-nine years old.

It was November 1943 and the Philippine Islands were experiencing the worst monsoon season in memory. The rainy season the year before had been blessedly light, with only five inches of precipitation. But in 1943 the monsoons had returned with a vengeance and produced thirty-seven inches of rain in one month. The rain had come at a time when her morale was low, and the damp, humid weather only added to her despair.

She had been a prisoner of the Japanese for almost two years at that point, living in squalid conditions, worrying constantly about the health of her husband and children. She recalled that the rain and wind was particularly bad on that November day, yet she fled the crowded dormitory building to spend time alone in the shanty Danny, her husband, had built for the family. She sat on the edge of the makeshift bed and watched the rain come down, hoping that the palm leaf roof would hold up. Their scanty belongings were being soaked by the wind gusts that had already blown rain water into the shanty.

She had done her best to protect the food stock, their most precious possession. As usual, her stomach was churning from hunger. She thought about the last nourishing meal she had eaten. Danny and she had brought the boys to her parent's house for dinner the night before they registered at Santo Tomas, January 18, 1942. They had feasted on roast beef, potatoes, vegetables, and one of her mother's delicious chocolate cakes. Almost two years had passed since she had eaten that meal; now she could barely imagine what it felt like to have a full stomach.

Her parents had left the camp in a prisoner exchange just two months prior and she was glad that they had not had to suffer through such a trying period. She had no idea where they were, or if they were safe, and she worried about them endlessly. Her intention to keep a diary for them to document her experiences after they left had been derailed by her hunger and low morale. She tortured herself with thoughts of how Danny and she might have escaped imprisonment if they had made different decisions.

She moved to the stoop of the shanty during a respite in the rain and watched her fellow inmates walk by along the muddy pathways. She observed internees who had been the cream of Manila's society reduced to hauling buckets of waste water to the nearby trough, dressed in worn and ragged clothing. Other prisoners took advantage of the sunshine to hang their wash on the nearby rope strung up between two posts. It was always necessary for the internees to wait while their clothes dried since clothes were often stolen.

Kathleen's thoughts were jarred back to the present day by the loud ring of the telephone. A friend needed a fourth for a bridge game later in the week and she was only too happy to accept the invitation. She was ninety now, and was fortunate to have so many friends to help her pass the days. She slowly got up from her chair to put the bridge date on her calendar and tightly gripped her walker as she headed to her office. She passed the picture of her mother and father hanging in the gallery as she traveled down the hallway. She paused to look at her father, Thomas.

Thomas had been an interesting man, far ahead of his time in many respects. He was an adventurer at heart; it was because of him that the family had moved to the Philippines. She slowly progressed down the hall to the bedroom she used as her office. She eased down onto the padded desk chair and made a note of the bridge date on her schedule.

Kathleen put her pen down and glanced at the cabinet beside her desk that held her library of books. She had a large collection of books written by people with whom she had been interned in Santo Tomas. She had planned to write her own story of the camp experience after she was released, but somehow work and family responsibilities had always taken precedence. She often imagined what she would have written if she had found the time for it. She eased back into the chair and gazed out the window. She began to envision the book she would write about Santo Tomas.

1

The Glorious East

As a girl growing up in the Philippines I loved everything about America. It seemed as far away and exotic to me as the moon. My girlfriends and I rushed to the newsstand each month when the shipment of American magazines came in, filled with stories of movie stars and the latest fashions. We couldn't get enough of them. We imagined the excitement of viewing a Broadway show or a concert at Carnegie Hall. I dreamt of leaving the Philippines some day to attend college in the United States. I longed to visit Washington, D.C. and Boston to see the places described in my school books. I wanted to *be* an American.

Technically, I was half-American, as my father had been raised in Boston, but even he had not seen the United States for more than twenty years by the time I came along. Dad had been born under fortunate circumstances in 1873. He was an only child, but part of an extended family of cousins in a tight knit, conservative clan residing in the "Hub." Dad's father died when he was only eleven, and although he and my grandmother were well provided for, his childhood was shattered by the loss. To ease his pain he took up piano and tennis and soon became proficient at both.

Dad attended local preparatory schools, after which my grandmother gave him the choice of enrolling at Harvard or at Massachusetts Institute of Technology. His decision was based on pure emotion; his least favorite cousin was attending Harvard so Dad decided to enroll at MIT. He knew that a career and marriage were expected of him but he was bored by the offers he received from the local accounting firms; he yearned for adventure and excitement before settling down. He suggested a world tour to his mother, with her along as chaperone, and she readily agreed. His intention was to remain in their last tour stop, Berlin, to study music before returning home.

Dad and my grandmother set off on their journey from New York City in the fall of 1894, traveling by train to Los Angeles. Once there, they spent time visiting the ocean and riding horses on a nearby ranch before boarding a ship bound for the

Orient. After a long voyage, they berthed in Shanghai and toured the city before proceeding on to Japan, where they found the country and the people enchanting. My father's grand plans came to an abrupt halt; he decided to go no farther.

Dad secured a job teaching English at Kayo University in Tokyo. He was in the prime of his life and enthusiastically immersed himself in the customs of the Japanese. He learned the language quickly and was fluent within a matter of months. The students at Kayo were unfamiliar with tennis so he equipped them with racquets and balls and taught them the game. His role as a teacher put him in a revered class and he was honored when he was invited to be introduced to the Emperor. Many years later this distinction would play a pivotal role in his life.

My grandmother died of cancer during Dad's tenure at Kayo. He left Tokyo shortly after her death and ventured out to see more of the country. He visited Yokohama, settled in to a new job at the local university, and met my mother, Dora Talbot.

My mother was the daughter of an English mother, who died when she was young, and an Irish father who headed the Far East operations for Equitable Life Insurance Company. They led a privileged life, living in China and Tokyo, before settling in Yokohama. I don't know when my father and mother met, but they did not have a whirlwind courtship. They were engaged for over a year before they were finally married in April 1909. They produced two children in short order: my sister Doreen was born in 1910 and my brother, Thomas Jr. (Tommy) was born in 1912.

In 1913 Dad's tennis club selected him to represent them at a tennis tournament in Manila. Once there, Dad saw a burgeoning city with an air of excitement that ran through the population. Americans were evident in every walk of life and their influence was attractive to him. He was certain that Manila was a place where he could merge his American background and education with his love for the Orient. He went home, packed up the family, and moved to the Philippines. His timing was perfect; Manila was on the verge of a cultural and economic boom.

The peace treaty signed after the end of the Spanish-American War in 1898 transferred governance of the Philippines from Spain to the United States. The U.S. intended to govern the Philippines indefinitely but the U.S. Congress amended the terms of the peace treaty in 1902 providing for transition to Philippine self-rule in 1946. Spain had ruled the Philippines for more than 300 years and its influence was apparent in Manila's architecture and culture, but in order for the Philippines to become a sovereign nation, sound financial and political bases had to be established.

In 1903 the United States began to prepare the Philippines for their independence. The U.S. military immediately embarked on developing the Philippines into a strategic military site. Manila was the main focus of modernization and development. Located on the western shore of Luzon, the northernmost of the Philippine's 7,000-island archipelago, Manila had a natural bay that was ideal for both military and commercial shipping.

The American governor of the Philippines lured major corporations and international trading companies to Manila. The companies soon began constructing office buildings in the new business district. Libby's Foods, National City Bank of New York [now Citigroup], Firestone Tires, United Artists, General Electric, International Harvester, and U. S. Steel were just some of the companies that established a presence in Manila. A thriving stock exchange was established as a result of the new economic vitality that Manila enjoyed. British expatriates were sent to the Philippine Islands as representatives of the vast trade industry that was present in Asia at the time.

As the Americans turned their attention to raising the level of education, English became the adopted language of the islands. The Americans knew that a literate population was crucial to self-government and economic security. Traditionally only the upper-class Filipinos had attended school, usually private parochial institutions. The Americans established public schools that brought education to every strata of Filipino society. Hundreds of teachers from the U.S. moved to the Philippines to participate in the first secular school system.

In 1912, just months before my father relocated the family to Manila, the United States and the Philippines signed an agreement allowing for unrestricted free trade between the two countries. The impact of the agreement bolstered the Philippine economy through large agricultural exports to the U.S. At the same time, the American military was establishing bases near Manila, in Subic Bay, which was becoming a major anchorage for the U.S. naval fleet. All of this development and building resulted in a booming job market.

When our family arrived in Manila in 1913 Dad was immediately hired as an accountant for the United States Navy. His new job had the added benefit of military housing in Cavite, a town near the naval base, where the family moved into a small but comfortable home. In February 1914 I was born, and that summer my parents moved the family into a big, rambling house in a suburb of Manila known as Santa Mesa. The house was on Sociego Street, where we lived for five years, surrounded by other expatriate families.

The European and American expatriate communities were playing a large part in building the "new" Manila. In turn, we enjoyed a privileged and luxurious lifestyle that would have been impossible to achieve in our native countries. Servants, from maids and cooks to *amahs* (nannies) and laundry women, were abundant and cheap. One did not need to be wealthy to live what Americans would have considered an upper class lifestyle. Days were played out with a tropical, slow-paced elegance.

Lavish parties were held at the Manila Hotel, one of the finest hotels in the world. Orchestras played nightly on its dance floor, open on one side to Manila Bay's sparkling waters. The Manila Hotel's bar was a gathering place for guests to view the multi-hued sunsets while sipping cocktails from the hotel's bar.

Expatriates formed clubs of all sorts, catering to every activity and nationality: Army-Navy for the military; Elks and Masons, primarily for Americans; St. Andrews Society for the Scots; the exclusive Manila Club for the British; and sporting clubs for polo and yachting. Entertainment districts with night clubs and theaters sprang up, golf courses were built, and lush public parks with meandering walking paths and tennis courts were opened for the enjoyment of all. Contemporary American culture was imported through movies and the 500,000 copies of magazines that were flown each month to the Philippines from the U.S.

Dad loved working with the ever-expanding Navy in Manila, but by 1919 he needed more money to support the family. His financial needs, combined with his love of travel and adventure, led him to seek another position. In 1920 he accepted a job as the accountant for a sugar plantation on the southern Philippine island of Negros. Our life on the plantation was a far cry from the cosmopolitan atmosphere we were used to in Manila. The compound consisted of eight families, an office, and a commissary. The only social life was playing bridge in the evenings and even that was curtailed because the lights were turned off at nine o'clock to keep expenses down. There were no schools, so Mother undertook home schooling Doreen, Tommy and me. In 1921 we welcomed a new member of the family, my brother Jack.

In 1922, the sugar plantation folded due to inadequate funding and our family moved back to our old Santa Mesa neighborhood where we reveled in "civilization"—grocery stores, theaters, abundant shopping and schools. I began attending the Central School, a public school that was provided by the federal government for those children whose fathers were American. We were a racially mixed crew, since many American soldiers had remained after the Spanish-American War and had married Filipino women. I loved my teachers and made great efforts to please them. My report cards reflected this; I was described as good student and obedient. I made many friends at Central School, some of whom were Filipino. While we shared friendships during school hours, after school we went our separate ways; I returned to the all-white expatriate community while they went to their homes on the other side of the city. It never occurred to us to socialize outside of school.

Like young girls everywhere I couldn't wait to enter high school, a place where I anticipated more challenging school work and an exciting social life. I wasn't disappointed. My senior year in high school was one of the best years of my life, with parties and academic endeavors keeping me very busy. People told me that I was attractive; I think it is always hard to judge that sort of thing about one's self, but I suspect that my light curly hair and crystalline blue eyes stood out among my schoolmates who were of Spanish extraction. I had an active social life, with a steady stream of suitors asking me for dates. My days were filled with festivities: dances, parties, the class play, and finally, graduation. It was a solemn occasion, the culmination of an era. Nothing was ever quite the same after that.

The Chapman family sits for a formal portrait in 1931.
From top row left, Tommy, Jack and Thomas. On the bottom row, from left, are Doreen, Dora and Kathleen.

I desperately wanted to attend college but the money for such a luxury was scarce. It was 1932, the height of the Depression, and the money required to travel to the United States and subsist for four years on my own was simply not there. I lobbied my parents to allow me to live with Dad's relatives in Boston, but they pointed out that the only relatives we had were distant cousins who had never laid eyes on me. The only path open to me was to enroll at the Insular Business College near our home where I could gain the skills necessary to get a job. I studied hard during the day but made the most of my free time by attending beach parties, dinners and dances. I even took a turn at acting in the local theater company.

One Sunday in 1934 I was invited by some friends to join them for a picnic at the beach. I had been out late the night before and was torn between sleep and joining them. Tired, but afraid of missing out on the fun, I arose unwillingly. My lack of enthusiasm showed in my outfit; I wore old basketball shorts and a white gym shirt. I walked to the beach to meet my friends and was sitting on the bed of a friend's truck when we were approached by two of our school friends and a stranger. They introduced us to the stranger, a young Scotsman who had recently moved to Manila. I jumped down off the truck, ripping my shorts in the process, and shook the hand of my future husband, Danny Watson.

Daniel Jackson Watson was the youngest of six children, born to a surgeon and his wife in Glasgow, Scotland. He graduated from college with a degree in accounting and went to work for an old British import/export firm, Ker and Co. He spent the first few years of his career traveling to China, Jakarta, Japan, Thailand and Malaysia. Danny was tall, with a wry sense of humor, quick intelligence and well-liked by everyone who met him. He reveled in the opportunity he'd had to see the world, although he missed fly fishing in Scotland. He joined the Manila office of Ker and Co. in 1934 and soon thereafter was convinced to join his friends on that memorable picnic.

Danny and I knew from the start that we were meant for each other. Danny asked me to marry him a few weeks after our first meeting and I eagerly agreed. We had such big plans for the future! Ker and Co., on the other hand, had very old-fashioned ideas. One was that their male employees be paid so little that they couldn't afford to marry. It was a practice that many British firms embraced. Their position was that if the employee failed in his overseas assignment it was simpler to send home a single man than a whole family. So, of necessity our engagement was a long one. For two years we scrimped and saved. Danny bunked with other bachelors in small rooms while I lived at home with my family, and worked as a secretary at the Goodyear Tire Company.

As I think back about that time I am struck by the parallels between the changes and growth in my own life and those occurring in the Philippines. It was an eventful time for everyone. Manila had grown into a lively, bustling city by 1935. The economy and infrastructure had taken hold more quickly than had been anticipated in 1902. The Philippine President, Manuel Quezon, was convinced that the country was ready to be independent of the United States. Quezon traveled to Washington to meet with President Franklin Roosevelt to begin negotiations for an early transition to self-rule.

Quezon knew that one of Roosevelt's chief concerns about an independent Philippine nation was the inadequacy of the Filipino military. Both Roosevelt and Quezon were well aware of the Philippines' strategic location, not only for the United States but increasingly for Japan as well. Japan had conquered Manchuria in 1931 and was threatening to occupy more territory in Asia. The Japanese had developed an economic and political program, the "Greater East Asia Co-Prosperity Sphere," which was aimed at liberating Asia from the control of Western nations. The Philippine Islands were squarely in the middle of the territory that the Japanese intended to liberate. Both Quezon and Roosevelt knew the Philippines needed a military that could repel the Japanese should conflicts arise.

Quezon asked Roosevelt to appoint General Douglas MacArthur to the Philippines in order to devise a defense strategy. MacArthur's father had been stationed in Manila during the Spanish-American War and was considered a hero for his actions during that conflict. Quezon suspected that MacArthur would relish the opportunity to return to the country of his childhood where his father was held in such high regard. President Roosevelt, eager to get the always-controversial MacArthur out of Washington, eagerly complied with Quezon's request. MacArthur, along with his aide, Dwight Eisenhower, moved to Manila in 1935.

MacArthur thrived in the adoration showered on him by the Filipinos. He was made a Field Marshal of the Army of the Philippines, a somewhat meaningless position by American standards but one of great status in Manila. MacArthur checked his family into the Manila Hotel, where they lived in grandeur, their every need anticipated and fulfilled. MacArthur and Eisenhower divided their time between developing defense plans and asking Quezon and Roosevelt for money. Between 1935 and 1941 they never received all the funds they felt necessary to construct an adequate defense system. They planned as best they could with the capital they were allotted.

Danny and I, like most expatriates in Manila, were unaware of the work that MacArthur and his staff were doing. We saw the General at a few of the formal functions we attended but those occasions were always social in nature where military matters were not discussed. We spent most evenings during our courtship quietly playing cards and enjoying music with my parents. Frequently we would see the latest movie imported from America and then rush to the Manila Hotel to dance under the stars. On Sundays we often traveled to the mountain city of Baguio, where Danny played polo for the Scottish team.

Danny and I were finally able to afford marriage in 1936. We were married in June in a quiet ceremony at the Cathedral of St. Mary and St. John. We moved to a little cottage near my parent's house on Sociego Street and saved with a new goal in mind: Scotland. Danny was anxious to introduce me to his family and was due a trip home from his company. But once again, Ker and Co. would not acknowledge a spouse. They would pay for Danny's expenses to return home on leave, but not mine. Nature intervened before we could save enough money for the trip. In August, 1937, we were thrilled to welcome our first son, Richard. I remember thinking that life seemed so complete then; we had friends, work and finally, a baby to love.

Danny and Kathleen on their wedding day, June 20, 1936.

By early 1938 we had saved enough money for the journey home to Scotland. It was literally a "slow boat" for much of the trip—36 days in all from Manila to London. Another trip by train landed us at the doorstep of Danny's family in Glasgow. The trip was quite exhausting. Prior to World War II, travel to Europe was not the easy matter that it is today; it was all done by ship and was a lengthy and costly business.

When we got to Scotland, it was quite an ordeal meeting so many strangers. I don't think anyone in the family had ever met an American before and I'll never know just what they expected. Moreover, I had come from some remote island in the Pacific! I think the change in culture was as much of a shock to me, but luckily I was young and adaptable. And after all, we did speak the same language! We visited the home in Strathaven that had housed generations of Watsons. I was convinced that I was in the coldest house in the coldest town in Scotland. In addition, I was overwhelmed by the care Richard required. I was accustomed to tropical temperatures and servants and felt that I couldn't possibly be further removed from my normal surroundings.

In September, 1938, we had the dubious excitement of being in Britain at the time of the Munich Accord. Britain's Prime Minister Neville Chamberlain was in Munich to meet with Adolf Hitler, Italy's Prime Minister, Benito Mussolini, and French Premier Edouard Daladier to reach an agreement regarding Germany's invasion of Czechoslovakia. It was hoped that an appeasement of Hitler on the Czech issue would stop any further advancement by the Nazi leader. Hitler had already invaded Austria; a successful resolution regarding Czechoslovakia was critical to the safety and security of the remainder of Europe.

Everyone in Britain at that time, including Danny and me, hung over the radio waiting with tension and dread for some word from Chamberlain. He eventually returned from Munich, triumphantly declaring that Hitler had agreed to "peace in our time". Of course, that promise only lasted another year. On September 1, 1939 Hitler invaded Poland and World War II began. I often wonder what our fate might have been had Chamberlain not secured the "peace". Might we have stayed on in Europe and saved ourselves the horrendous years to follow?

It was a moot point. In January 1939 we left Britain and began our journey back home to the Philippines. We set foot in Manila forty-five days later, tired and exhausted from the trip but very happy to be home. I was thrilled to see my parents and Danny enthusiastically resumed his work at Ker and Co. Richard was back in the care of his *amah*, allowing me to resume my leisurely existence. Danny and I re-kindled old friendships and our social life took off where we had left it. We enjoyed dinner parties, bridge games, and picnics with other young families on the weekends.

To us, the war in Europe seemed very far away, something we would have been concerned about had we remained in Scotland. We felt insulated from the world's problems living in the remote American commonwealth of the Philippine Islands. Like people the world over, most of us in Manila found it more pleasant to think about everyday life than the looming prospect of war. Hopes were high in the expatriate community that tensions elsewhere in the world would be eased and our way of life would go on as it always had.

Our fervent desire for the status quo existed despite the recent victories Japan had secured in China. American and British arrogance led most of us to believe that while the Chinese may have succumbed to the Japanese Army, the Japanese could not win any engagement with the superior Allied forces. We also had great confidence in Douglas MacArthur. President Roosevelt had promoted MacArthur to commander in chief of all U.S. military forces in the Far East in 1940. MacArthur had already gone on record concerning the defense of the Philippines in a 1936 *Collier's Magazine* article, stating, "We're going to make it so very expensive for any nation to attack these islands that no one will try it." Our overconfidence may have been misplaced, but I believe it was understandable.

Like young couples everywhere, Danny and I focused on our family and our plans for the future. We rented a bigger house on Sociego Street, next to my parents. We began to think about expanding our family. We were optimistic about life, even if some around us were not. When I consulted our family physician about my readiness for a new baby, my query was met with a serious admonition: the doctor told me that it was no time to bring a child into the world. I told him that I did not intend to go through life with only one child. I must admit that had I known what lay ahead I might have changed my mind.

Our second child, Alan, was born in May, 1941. Blond-haired and blue-eyed, he looked exactly like me. Danny and I thought life could not be better; we had a new house, new baby, and a bright four-year old,. We enjoyed a leisurely summer, socializing and planning for another trip to Scotland to show off our new baby.

In September I was unexpectedly approached by the United States High Commissioner's office and offered a secretarial job for $140 per month. Such a high salary was unheard of in those days. I was reluctant to leave Alan at such a young age, but the job was presented to me on the grounds that it was my patriotic duty and temporary. I didn't know how temporary it would turn out to be.

I accepted the new job and began work in late September. By then, there was growing recognition in Manila that a war between the United States and Japan seemed inevitable. Japan had occupied the former French colonies of Indochina and hostilities were heating up all across Asia. A group of U. S. businessmen in Manila formed the American Coordinating Committee, aimed at developing contingency plans in the event war came to the Philippines. Still, most of us in the Philippine expatriate community had great faith in the U.S. Navy. If war came, we thought, it would be somewhere "out there" in the Pacific.

Kathleen with Richard (left) and Alan (right) in 1941.

The first Sunday in December in the Philippines was December 6. It was a day like any other day; we spent it with family and friends. In fact, as we read the *Manila Tribune* newspaper on Monday morning, December 7, we were encouraged by an article that reported negotiations between Tokyo and Washington were going well. We dressed for work, kissed the boys good-bye and set off for what we assumed would be a normal day. Because of the time difference we had no knowledge of the attack on Pearl Harbor.

I arrived at the High Commissioner's building to find workers unhurriedly piling sand bags around the perimeter. I couldn't imagine why we would be tak ing such precautions. When I asked the workers why they were fortifying the building, the laconic response was, "Oh, mum, the Japanese have bombed Pearl Harbor." I rushed into my office, shocked and uncertain, and found my co-workers numbly walking the halls, not knowing what was expected of them.

Everything seemed suddenly changed. The day before had been filled with fun activities, playing with the children, and socializing with friends. Twenty-four hours later I found myself crouched under my desk for an air raid drill. Amidst the confusion my boss announced that the office would be moved to Baguio. Baguio traditionally had been the summer capital of the Philippines; it's location in the mountains a relief from the heat and humidity of Manila. Later that morning we received word that Baguio had already been bombed. War had come to the Philippines.

Once started, the war came fast and furiously. On December 8, the Japanese flew over the city in perfect formation, but Manila was not the target. They proceeded to Clark Field, the home of the United States Army Air Corps in the Philippines, and destroyed much of it. In a scenario resembling the ships at Pearl Harbor, all the airplanes were on the ground, wing to wing. The people of Manila were as surprised as the residents of Honolulu had been the day before. On December 9 the Japanese hit Cavite and the naval base at Subic Bay, completely destroying both and killing over 1500 people.

Manila was bombed steadily over the next few days. The High Commissioner's office was constantly under attack. My desire to be home with the boys became paramount as the bombs fell all around me,. I quickly wrote a letter of resignation; a letter that would eventually cost me three years of salary.

More than 200,000 of the 600,000 people living in Manila had evacuated the city by mid-December, most heading for the rugged countryside. Danny and I felt safe. After all, Francis Sayre, the U.S. High Commissioner, and his family were still in Manila. We soon realized that our sense of security was misplaced. On December 24, MacArthur, Quezon, Sayre and their staffs fled Manila for Corregidor. We were unaware that this move to the fortress on "the Rock," as Corregidor was known, had been planned all along.

When MacArthur began devising the defense strategy for the Philippines in 1935, he knew that it would be nearly impossible to protect an archipelago of some 7,000 islands. He presumed, correctly, that Luzon would be the main island of attack and made plans accordingly. When the attack came his troops would retreat to Bataan while he and his command staff occupied Corregidor. They were to defend those positions while awaiting the arrival of aid from the

United States. The fortress on Corregidor was a marvel of modern planning, equipped with food, fuel, water, ammunition and other essential provisions.

The fatal flaw in MacArthur's plan was the almost complete devastation of the United States naval fleet at Pearl Harbor. The destruction of the fleet meant that there were no ships available to send to the rescue of the Philippines. Without aid from the United States, MacArthur did not have the men or equipment necessary to fend off the larger, more organized Japanese invasion force. The lack of adequate funding from the Philippine and United States governments had finally taken its toll.

An acting High Commissioner was left in charge of providing guidance to the American citizens living in the Philippines after MacArthur and Sayre moved to Corregidor. The Commissioner was appointed to provide the illusion of American stability, which was important to those of us looking for leadership in an uncertain time. His appointment was also seen as a way to keep the Filipinos loyal and negate any perception of desertion as the military moved to Corregidor. As it turned out, the Commissioner provided little direction and we soon realized that civilians of all nationalities, including us, were without protection from either the United States military or government.

The bombing around Manila continued steadily for the next few days and the noise and confusion continued around Clark Field. Two of Danny's friends who were stationed there came by to say their farewells as they went off to war and we never saw them again. It was a sad and somber Christmas, one we barely celebrated. The protection of the military was gone and in its place was a gnawing uncertainty about the future.

Danny and I were only confident of one thing—we were trapped in the Philippines with no clear means of escape to either the United States or Britain. MacArthur declared Manila an "open city" on December 26, allowing the Japanese to enter the city without resistance from the Allied forces. Although Tokyo acknowledged the declaration and the Japanese Army observed it, the Japanese Air Force continued to attack the city mercilessly. I was scared and worried about whether I could protect Richard and Alan from the incessant bombings.

The acting High Commissioner sent word to all expatriates on New Year's Day that the Japanese were going to enter Manila. He requested that all Allied civilians stay indoors and remain calm. Danny ignored the directive and made a dash down to his office to retrieve all of our family's important papers, including birth certificates and passports, as well as some cash that he kept in his safe.

We weren't sure why we were so desperate for our travel documents. We weren't sure where we would go, or even *if* we would be able to leave the country, but we wanted to be prepared. On Danny's way home, he observed chaos in the streets and widespread panic among some of the local population. I waited nervously for him at home, fearing that he would be shot by the Japanese. When Danny finally came through the front door, I breathed a sigh of relief. We began to sit and wait; there was no place to go.

The Japanese military entered the city on January 2. Roars of delight and revelry were heard throughout our neighborhood as they marched down our street. The uproar emanated from a house very near ours that was occupied by some Japanese men. After the attack on Pearl Harbor, the United States authorities in Manila had placed these men under house arrest. There was good reason for this, as the Japanese had been sending military men to Manila to act as spies since 1934. Colonels and majors were disguised as gardeners, bicycle salesmen, photographers and assorted tradesmen. Their purpose was to discover as much as possible about American military strength and strategy and relay it back to Japan. Some of these Japanese officers were living in the house near us where the celebration was taking place.

As their shouting and laughter continued, all of the expatriates in the neighborhood became more frightened. The Japanese Army's infamous behavior in China was well known; they had burned people alive, beheaded countless civilians, cut fetuses out of pregnant women, and raped for the sport of it. Their activities were still very fresh in our minds and we feared that our celebrating neighbors might seek revenge on us in a similar fashion. I still recall 60 years later that the experience was so horrifying that I have never again felt as terrified. The night passed without incident, but it was not quiet for long.

We spent every waking hour listening to the radio, waiting for some guidance from the government. Finally, two days after the Japanese marched into Manila, the acting High Commissioner announced that all enemy aliens were going to be rounded up for questioning. We were to wait at home until the Japanese came for us. The inference of the message was that we would be interned for a few days, asked to complete a perfunctory registration process, and then be allowed to return home. Relief flooded through the neighborhood.

Danny and I packed what we thought was necessary and then began a nerve-wracking period of waiting. We jumped each time a car door slammed shut on our street. We waited for several days, but still no Japanese came to our door. My brother, Tommy, had been working at the naval base in Cavite and was picked up by the Japanese while walking home from work. He was being held in one of the large detention areas in the center of the city.

Danny and I were relieved when on January 18 we read in the *Manila Tribune*, now being published by the Japanese, that all enemy aliens who had not yet been interned were to give themselves up. We were instructed to report to Santo Tomas University, and to bring enough food and clothing for three days. What a bitter joke those instructions turned out to be.

We were familiar with Santo Tomas. It was an old and revered university, the second oldest outside of Europe. It had been founded by Dominican Fathers in1611 to disseminate information about Christianity and European culture to the Filipino population. Over the years it had grown both in size and stature, and the elite of Filipino society all claimed Santo Tomas as their alma mater.

Classes at the university had ceased on December 8 with the outbreak of war, and the following week the U.S. Army took over the campus for use as a motor pool. On December 26, after MacArthur ordered the evacuation of the U.S. military to Corregidor, the American Red Cross obtained permission to use the campus as an internment camp. The first group of civilians entered the gates on January 4, 1942, and Santo Tomas Internment Camp officially began. Residents who had already been detained in holding areas dispersed across the city were all brought to Santo Tomas. We learned that Tommy was one of the prisoners who had been transferred there. His wife, Lolita, unable to support herself and their young daughter Carol on her own, had joined him inside Santo Tomas.

On January 19, Danny and I, along with Richard and Alan, gathered in front of our house. My parents, my brother Jack, and sister Doreen, joined us and we piled into Danny's car. Our faithful Filipino chauffeur drove us the short distance to Santo Tomas. Our car pulled up to the gate and we disembarked, joining the long line of people waiting to be processed by the Japanese officials. Some of our group would get a temporary reprieve; some would never see home again.

2

Protective Custody

The campus of Santo Tomas covered a square block, surrounded on each side by a major street. On three sides were tall, cement walls that served as perfect barriers for holding prisoners. The fourth side was graced by intricate iron fencing and a large main gate. At the center of the campus was the imposing Main building, five stories high, with elaborate architecture, a large balcony and a clock tower. The Annex, Education, Gymnasium, and Hospital buildings surrounded the Main building. Lawns and gardens had been cultivated by the Dominican order, providing the campus with a lush, tropical feel. On any other day, we considered the campus an ideal spot for a picnic.

We were among hundreds of wary American and British citizens waiting outside the main gate of Santo Tomas on that warm day in January 1942. Most of us carried baskets of food and a small valise of clothing to last us for the three days we expected to remain in custody. There was no class distinction in the line; a prosperous CEO stood next to the lowest manager in his company. We were all under the illusion that we would submit to a bureaucratic registration process and then be released to go home.

We waited for an hour outside the main gate. Finally, the Japanese guards approached us and told us to proceed to the Main building for processing. As we entered the building we found that Americans were separated from the British and the men were separated from the women and children. Thus, we were separated accordingly; the children and I were considered British because Danny was British but my parents and the rest of my family were placed in the American lines.

Each line, whether by nationality or gender, occupied space on a different floor of the building. It made little difference what floor one was on as each group waited *hours* to be processed. The rooms were warm and stuffy and unusually quiet, save crying children, as each person contemplated what the next few days might bring.

Every member of the family inched his or her way to the front of the line and submitted to the questions posed by the Japanese official. We were all asked perfunctory questions such as age, occupation, reason for being in Manila, etc. I watched the line ahead of me and saw many women I knew being told that they would need to remain in Santo Tomas for further questioning. It appeared that others were being allowed to return home. I couldn't discern any rhyme or reason as to why some had to stay and some were released.

When I reached the Japanese official for questioning he seemed particularly interested in how old Richard and Alan were. Immediately after I told him their ages he told me to return home and wait for further instructions. Apparently the Japanese guards on my floor already had their fill of crying babies and rambunctious toddlers. I breathed a sigh of relief and hoped that Danny would be allowed to return home as well.

I met the family outside the Main building at the end of the day and we shared our experiences. I had heard from several friends that most of the males under age 50 were being interned but I was still hopeful about Danny's fate. As he crossed the plaza in front of the building I knew immediately from his expression, that like most male "enemy aliens," he would remain in custody. I was crestfallen. To make matters worse, Jack and Doreen also had to stay.

My parents stood silently listening to our stories. Finally, my father told us of his experience and we stared at him in disbelief as he told his story. He had been approached while standing in line by a Japanese officer who asked, "Are you not Mr. Chapman?" When my father confirmed his identity, the soldier said, "Don't you remember me? I was your pupil forty years ago!" The soldier had been one of Dad's English students at Kayo University. Then as now, the Japanese have great reverence for both age and teachers. The fact that Dad had once been introduced to the Emperor also put him in an exalted class. He was a man to be respected, even in war. The officer expedited Dad's registration, rescued my mother from the women's line, and told them to return home.

Although separation was not our first choice, Danny and I were relieved that I would be able to return home with the boys. The campus was teeming with people and we knew that keeping two young children in tow under those circumstances would be difficult. Plus, nothing in the registration process led us to believe that we would be separated for more than the anticipated three days. My parents and I, along with Richard and Alan, left for home only to find that in the few short hours we had been away our households had experienced some unexpected changes.

I entered our house, tired, hot and unhappy over Danny's confinement. The children were very cranky and hungry. As I called out for our cook, I was met by Alan's *amah,* Irene, who informed me that all of our other servants had left us. The Japanese had warned the Filipino population not to associate with Allied civilians and that any infractions of that order would be met with harsh punishment. Understandably, few of the servants employed by the Allied expatriates were willing to risk the punishment. In reality, particularly at the beginning of the war, the Japanese did not enforce the order, but the threat alone was enough to scare off all but the most loyal of servants.

I slumped down onto a chair, completely overwhelmed by the events of the day. Suddenly I was alone and in need of a quick education in basic household tasks. Like other women of my age and upbringing, I had never learned how to do the most basic housekeeping or how to drive a car. Over the next few days I set about learning to cook and clean with fierce determination. I found it dreary and monotonous, but better than the imagined horrors of Santo Tomas.

Danny was experiencing a culture shock of his own. More than 2,000 people were interned in Santo Tomas and truckloads of new internees were arriving each day. Santo Tomas had traditionally been a commuter school with very few dormitory rooms, and the Japanese had done nothing to prepare the university as an internment camp. Each internee was assigned to either the Main building or the Annex where they scrambled through the rooms to claim a space to sleep.

The internees discovered that cots and blankets were in short supply and mosquito netting, a necessity in the tropics, was even scarcer. Some skeptical internees had correctly anticipated the need for bedding and had brought light blankets and pillows with them from home. These prescient people were few and far between. Most internees scurried from one building to the next, scrounging cots and bedding before nightfall. Not many were successful; the great majority ended up sleeping on the cement floors.

Protective Custody 19

An aerial view of Santo Tomas in the summer of 1945 after the U.S. Army had taken over the camp and removed the shanties. The large building in the center is the Main Building.
Photo courtesy of Dan Balkin.

Danny was surprised to hear that an internee governing structure had already been formed by the time he entered Santo Tomas. He also learned that the camp was being "managed" by civilian Japanese, mostly former diplomats and businessmen, who did not have the training or inclination to run a prisoner of war camp. The commandant of the camp had no desire to deal directly with the internees. He had demanded that they appoint a "general" with whom he could communicate and who, in turn, would be responsible for communicating to the internees.

Earl Carroll, an American businessman, was selected for the role as the liaison between the internees and the Japanese commandant. Carroll had been a member of the American Coordinating Committee prior to the outbreak of the war and was a familiar face to many of the prisoners. By the end of the first week of imprisonment, he had selected room leaders for each of the main sleeping rooms and had begun to take inventory of who was in camp and what provisions were available.

Carroll quickly formed a Central Committee (later called the "Executive Committee" and finally, the "Internee Committee") to identify the most immediate needs of the prisoners. He devised an organization structure with department heads to oversee such necessities as food, sanitation, and discipline. He authorized the re-opening of the former student cafeteria as a canteen to serve the needs of the internees.

The population of the camp mushroomed to 3,600 by February. The majority, more than 70 percent, were American. Another 25 percent were British, with the remainder made up of various European and Asian nationalities. Two thousand of the prisoners were men, more than 1,200 were women, and there were 400 children under the age of 15. Almost all of the internees were housed in the Main building and overcrowding became an immediate problem.

Each person staked out a small space in their assigned room and then jealously guarded against infringement from new arrivals. Sleeping arrangements became intolerable with 30–50 people in each room. People slept on cots, thin mattresses, or the cement floor. Danny was one of the lucky internees who found a cot. The inhabitants of the sleeping rooms found it impossible to move about without disrupting the clothing, personal items and bedding that covered every inch of the floor. A good night's sleep became impossible due to the noise, movement and poor bedding. The muggy, tropical climate also served to make the rooms stifling and uncomfortable.

The prisoners engaged in an increasing number of squabbles and disagreements as they became more sleep-deprived and as the quarters became more cramped. People argued about the smallest of problems and perceived slights. Long lines for the handful of bathroom stalls wound down the main hallways. There was no consideration shown for emergencies; everyone was required to keep their place in line no matter how dire their situation. Showers were taken in groups and were necessarily short. The internees soon considered modesty a luxury and self-consciousness went by the wayside quickly. There was no privacy and no time alone within the barracks. The situation was aptly described in a sign above the men's toilet area: "If you want privacy, close your eyes."

Danny discovered that the camp canteen was not stocked to feed the thousands of inhabitants in residence at Santo Tomas. The Japanese absolved themselves of responsibility for feeding the internees during the first six months of their captivity despite the obvious food shortage. The Japanese did not consider

Santo Tomas a prison camp; instead, they viewed themselves as benevolently holding the Allied civilians in "protective custody."

Regardless of the category, in reality the Japanese had no practice of providing food to their captives. In fact, their own troops were expected to forage for food wherever they were deployed in the Pacific and they expected the same foraging skills from the internees. However, the food situation the Japanese encountered in Manila was unlike any of the other territories they had occupied in the Pacific.

Looters had destroyed the city's stores of food a week before the Japanese entered the city, so there was no stockpile of goods to draw from once the local vendors' stores were depleted. Further complicating the problem was that the Philippines grew few crops and had depended upon other countries, primarily the United States, for their main source of food. The food supply lines were cut off with the outbreak of war, resulting in shortages from the start. At the beginning of 1942 it was estimated that there was just enough rice stored in Manila to last six months and enough sugar to last for 15 months.

Danny's assessment of the meals provided in the canteen was that they were meager by most anyone's standards. The cooks used corn mush, watery stews, rice, and native vegetables as the basis of the menu. The prisoners ate two meals a day, one in the morning and one in the evening, and for that they waited in line for as much as an hour. Danny often needed to pick worms and weevils out of his porridge to make it edible.

In February, the Japanese commandant acknowledged the food shortage and allowed the Philippine Red Cross to supply the prisoners with food, kitchen equipment, toilets, medical supplies, cots, sewing machines and clothing. But the Japanese imposed such bureaucratic hurdles that it took the Red Cross weeks to establish a consistent flow of aid. In the interim, a life-saving institution, the "package line," was born.

The prisoners' faithful Filipino servants, friends and family began lining up outside the main gate and fence at the front of the camp, pushing packages through the iron rails. The packages contained items that provided some level of comfort to the internee: food, clothing, bedding, medicine, and the like. Prisoners also exchanged notes and letters with those on the outside through the "package line," even though written correspondence was forbidden by the Japanese.

Prisoners could not go near the fence, but they could shout out requests to anyone who had come to see them. Internees with money passed it to their friends on the outside, with a list detailing what supplies were to be purchased with the funds. Similarly, internees who had little or no cash asked friends or servants to empty their bank accounts and pass the money back in to them through the "package line". As in any crisis, cash was king, especially at the beginning of the war when food and supplies were available for purchase.

The shouting, shoving and package exchanges soon rendered the fence area a madhouse. The Japanese were annoyed that the Filipinos, whom they had come to "rescue" from their Western oppressors, were loyal to the prisoners. On one day alone, thirty-five notes written between internees and their former servants were confiscated. The commandant was irate and threatened to prohibit all packages from entering the camp.

Earl Carroll was able to convince the commandant to retain the "package line" but he did so with some new provisos. The commandant required that the line be organized so that packages were sent through the main entry gate in an orderly manner and no longer shoved through the fence rails. Internees were also forbidden to speak with the people at the fence. The new rules were put in place; four tables were set up at the gate and each package was delivered to, and inspected by, a Japanese officer before being transported to a holding point in the middle of the campus and then handed to the internee.

The new structure of the "package line" meant that there were long lines to deliver any goods to the camp. It remained a crowded and difficult area to navigate. Some days I would go to the gate, take my place in line, and wait hours only to be told that the guards were done for the day so I would have to return home. I only managed to get a package in to Danny once a week.

We remained confident that the period of his internment would be short-lived. That confidence was not shaken when we learned in late March that MacArthur had been evacuated from Corregidor to Australia, uttering his famous promise of, "I shall return." We surmised that MacArthur would not have left his command in the Philippines unless Bataan and Corregidor were holding firm. Our spirits rose as rumors circulated that the U.S. would soon rescue us and this dreadful period would end.

We had no real perception of how events were playing out in the world, of course, owing to the lack of any independent newspaper or radio. The only media we received was the *Manila Tribune* and it was hardly an objective voice since the Japanese occupation. Consequently, all of us Allied civilians, both inside and outside of Santo Tomas, were completely taken aback when the Allied forces on Bataan surrendered to the Japanese on April 9.

A month later, the Japanese commandant took pleasure in announcing to the internees that Corregidor had been captured and that General Wainwright, the commander of the U.S. Forces in the Far East since MacArthur's departure, had instructed all U.S. troops in the Philippines to surrender. As a result, over 12,000

U.S. and 70,000 Filipino troops became POWs and began the infamous Bataan Death March to the Cabanatuan prison camp in northern Luzon. In Manila, hope for a speedy delivery died and a depression fell over the city. Civilians, both inside and outside of the camp, fell into a day-to-day waiting pattern.

In Santo Tomas, the internee's initial shock at the American surrender gradually wore off. The prisoners realized that their confinement would not be as short as they had hoped and resolved to improve their living conditions. The average internee had been a mid-to-high level executive of his company so it was an exceedingly motivated, highly educated group, not the kind to meekly accept its fate. The Executive Committee formed more sub-committees to oversee issues such as health, labor, family relations, gardening, entertainment and petty crime, utilizing many of the former executives as committee chairs. Food remained the primary concern, so the internees planted a garden that produced *camotes* (native sweet potatoes), beans, and *talinum* (a leafy, spinach-like plant).

Filipino and Japanese merchants established shops inside the gates, selling food, clothing, tools, books and other small luxuries such as soap. Aguinaldos, one of the most prestigious department stores in Manila, opened a branch in the Main building. Vendors set up stalls on the lawns of the campus selling hot dogs, ice cream, candy and tobacco. In the evenings lights were strung around the stalls, giving them the appearance of booths at a county fair.

The vendor's offerings were a blessing for some and torturous reminders for others. Internees who had lived and worked in Manila had access to money, either from their own resources or borrowed from friends. These fortunate internees were able to avail themselves of the wares being sold in camp and improve their living conditions. But many people in camp did not have money.

Expatriates who had lived on the outlying islands migrated to Manila when the war broke out, leaving all of their money in local banks. Many British internees had become stranded in the Philippines when they fled Singapore in advance of the Japanese occupation. They had boarded ships headed for India or Australia, but when Pearl Harbor was bombed their ships sought safe harbor in Manila and they were captured by the Japanese. People in both of these circumstances did not have resources or contacts in Manila, and whatever small amount of traveling money they possessed was depleted quickly when they first arrived. Without money, these internees were completely dependent upon the food and supplies allocated by the Executive Committee.

As the camp population grew, the Executive Committee wrestled with finding enough food to supply everyone. Finally, to stretch the Red Cross rations further, they encouraged those with money to forego the rations and purchase their food from one of the camp vendors. Danny was fortunate to have some money still in his possession so he could purchase food. I also sent small amounts of meat and vegetables in to him so that he ate as well as was possible under the circumstances.

Danny and I began to grapple with the very real possibility that our separation was going to last much longer than we had anticipated. The situation was very hard on us and the boys. I was struggling to run our household alone. I was living on the money Danny had salvaged from the safe on that dash to his office on New Year's Day, and it provided just enough for our immediate needs. Our expenses were growing at an alarming rate. I found it hard to find food from any source, and when it could be found, it came at a high price.

My friends and I had always had the luxury of ordering food over the phone with subsequent doorstep delivery. But phone service for all Allied citizens had been cut off and stores no longer delivered food to Allied citizens. At the age of 28 I ventured out to a local Filipino market for the first time in my life. I recall it as a bustling and crowded place, full of strange odors and native foods I had never seen before. My cooking became quite creative between the lack of money and the exotic foods.

I was constantly worried about medical problems, since I knew that all of the American and British doctors were interned in the camp. I was not worried about the absence of doctors for myself, but I was concerned about the possibility of Richard or Alan contracting a serious disease. I learned to handle emergencies as best I could and was comforted by my parents' presence next door.

In May, the Japanese began to exert their authority over the civilians outside the camp. I awoke one morning to find a contingent of Japanese military men on my doorstep. They entered the house and proclaimed that all of our household goods, including the car, were now property of the Japanese empire. The men spread out to every room, methodically placing seals on everything. The lieutenant of the group sat with me and we quietly conversed while my furniture and household goods were inventoried and labeled by the soldiers.

As the lieutenant and I talked he noticed my wedding portrait hanging on a nearby wall. "You were very beautiful then," he commented. I glanced at the picture with chagrin; it had been less than six years since my wedding day, but I knew then the toll the past few months had taken on my face. As they drove off in our car, Richard broke into hysterics, shouting "Please don't take my Daddy's car!" and there was little I could do to comfort him. Our life was beginning to change rapidly.

Danny and I did not see each other all of that spring. Our only form of communication was through notes smuggled inside the food baskets that I sent him and the laundry that he sent out to me. Inflation was unchecked and by June my money was running out. My parents were also running short of funds. A few of our neighbors sold jewelry and furniture for extra income. Unfortunately, my possessions had been designated as Japanese property and I did not have jewelry to sell, but I did have a secret source of cash.

After Pearl Harbor, a friend who had enlisted in the Navy asked Danny and me to hide his car from the Japanese and keep it until the war was over. It was fairly well hidden in my father's enclosed garage, but I knew that the Japanese were systematically searching all Allied property. I feared that it would only be a matter of time before the Japanese found and confiscated it. I decided that it was better to see some profit from the car than have it go to the Japanese, so when a local Filipino offered to buy it for $250 I took the offer. It was a great sum of money for that time and I knew it would go a long way toward feeding the family for another few months.

The problem was finding food to purchase. Those of us living on the outside were not beneficiaries of Red Cross provisions such as those provided to the internees. Everyone in Manila began to experience severe deprivation. In late July, deliverance came to me in a strange way. I looked out my window to see a Japanese man standing on the doorstep holding an official-looking paper. When I opened the door he began to read from the document: the house was needed for Japanese officers' quarters and I was to be out within the week. I had no choice but to join Danny in Santo Tomas.

The next week the Japanese sent a truck to transport Richard, Alan and me to the camp. I was told I could bring a few personal items with me, but nothing that was affixed with a Japanese seal. I recklessly ignored those instructions and grabbed anything I thought might offer some creature comfort in the camp. I dragged two rattan chairs, a table, a camphor-wood chest and an Oriental rug out to the waiting truck. The Japanese driver must have decided to ignore the labels as well as he helped me lift my reclaimed possessions on to his truck. I gave my silver and crystal to a Swiss friend to be stored in their neutral warehouse. Alan's faithful *amah*, Irene, the only servant who had not deserted us, cried as we drove off. We never saw her again.

The boys and I entered the camp to find daily life had been fairly well organized by the Executive Committee. We did not experience the confusion and lack of supplies that plagued Santo Tomas during its first few months of existence. By the time we moved to the camp in August, vendors and restaurants were up and running and the overcrowded conditions in the dormitories had been relieved by the advent of shanties.

Some industrious men built the first shanties in February. They were simple lean-to's built from scraps of scavenged wood and tin. The men constructed them wherever open space and flat land allowed so they were scattered all over the campus. When the spring rains came, many were ruined and others were washed away altogether. After Wainwright's surrender it became clear that the war would last longer than anticipated, and the men began to build more sophisticated shanties.

Filipino contractors brought construction materials in from the outside and sold them to the desperate prisoners for a handsome profit. Some internees hired professional Filipino contractors to build their shanties for them. Shanties were built out of native nipa palm leaves and bamboo; the nipa was used for roofs and the bamboo poles were used for framing and flooring. The internees spent an average of $75 to construct their shanties.

The Japanese were concerned that immoral activities would take place within the privacy of the shanties, so they required all shanties to have open sides with the interior clearly visible. People planted native flowers around the perimeter of the shanties in an attempt to make them seem homier.

Once Danny learned that the boys and I would be joining him in camp, he set about building a shanty that would fit our needs. I thought his efforts resulted in quite a superior structure. Our shanty was elevated and had three steps leading up to it to keep rain water out during the monsoon period. The sides were made of bamboo, with a nipa palm roof for shade. The addition of the table, chairs, rug, and chest that I brought from home made it a cozy retreat. Danny purchased a small bed to fit into one corner that provided comfort for Alan's afternoon naps. We ate dinner together in the shanty with food I cooked on a charcoal stove. Danny configured a sink out of a discarded five-gallon kerosene can, and that invention allowed us to clean our dishes in the shanty rather than the crowded central wash area.

Small "neighborhoods" of shanties began to spring up near each of the major buildings on campus. Danny chose the "Garden Court" area for our "home." It had once been the site of a dump, but some of the nicest shanties in camp were built there. Each of the neighborhoods elected a local mayor and chief of police, all of whom cooperated with the Executive Committee.

Those of us who lived in shanties improved the quality of our lives considerably. Even before we were allowed to sleep in them, we could cook, relax, play games, read, and most importantly, have private time with our family. Shanties also provided escape from the unrelenting noise and the pervasive ailments that were easily spread in the crowded buildings. These small things set shanty life apart from life in the barracks and gave us some sense of normalcy in an otherwise frenzied environment. The only inconvenience was that the Japanese forbade us from spending the night in the shanty, so each night after dinner Danny returned to the men's barracks to sleep while the boys and I were quartered in the Annex building.

The Annex was probably the worst building on the campus. It had been chosen, I believe, because it had a small kitchen and we were supposed to get slightly better food than that served to the rest of the camp. I was never convinced that was the case. There were about thirty women and children crowded into the room so there was a complete lack of privacy. We had to dress and undress with an audience, although I think we all grew quite callous about it. I shared a shower with one or two other women each time, always in cold water. I never got used to the shock of it hitting my skin, even in that tropical climate.

In September 1942 the Executive Committee decided that boredom and lack of activity was having a deleterious affect on camp morale. They declared that work detail was no longer voluntary; to keep us distracted and productive, each person was assigned a job. Socialites who had never lifted a finger were now required to scrub bathrooms, serve food, clean sleeping quarters, and the like. Danny was assigned to the carpentry shop where they made hundreds of wooden beds for those unlucky people who had nothing to sleep on I was assigned toilet duty, which meant sitting outside the toilets and wiping off the seats after each use. A year earlier I had never cleaned a house; now I was cleaning public toilets, often with Alan tucked under my arm.

The Committee organized schools for the children, staffed by teachers who were among the internee population. We adults were so starved for entertainment and relaxation that we eagerly looked forward to any sort of distraction. Subject matter experts were recruited from the camp population to teach adult classes in a wide array of subjects. Internees donated books for a library, organized bridge tournaments and formed baseball and football teams. A clever entertainer by the name of Dave Harvey put on shows each month on the outdoor stage constructed on the plaza in front of the Main building. Dave's shows provided us with much-needed levity, which was enhanced by watching our fellow internees take part in the skits.

Life went on in a monotonous, but busy, routine. Our main diversion was thinking about food; we became obsessed with food in ways I had not thought possible before our internment. The meals provided in the main food line were adequate but very dull, lacking in flavor and variety, and the food obtainable through the stalls in camp was limited and expensive.

By necessity I learned a great deal about primitive cooking. Our main cooking tool was the charcoal stove that Danny constructed with materials obtained from a camp vendor. Using a charcoal stove was very tedious since the charcoal had to be fanned constantly to attain the desired heat. I had to improvise cooking common dishes, such as bread, cakes and puddings, using the supplies that were available. We were delighted when we could get vegetables from the camp garden. Two years later we would look back at these meals with fondness, but at the time they were clearly inferior to the fare we had eaten before the war.

Danny and I were lucky in many respects. We still had some money from the friend's car I had sold that spring. My parents were able to send us small amounts of food from the outside, and Mother ensured that our laundry was done and sent to us via the "package line."

Occasionally I was allowed to obtain a pass to visit my parents. It was a wonderful distraction from everyday camp life and I eagerly looked forward to each outing. The Japanese were fairly lenient about issuing passes in the early days of the camp, especially if one had relatives on the outside. My brother Tommy generally accompanied me on these trips, adding to my enjoyment.

We were required to wear red armbands whenever we left Santo Tomas. Once, as Tommy and I were receiving our passes and arm bands, we were told the rules had changed and that a guard must go with us. When we arrived at my parent's home, I rushed up the stairs to warn my parents of our unexpected guest. Tommy followed with the guard, who politely bowed and drew up a chair as far away from the family as possible. When Mother served lunch, the guard moved to the table and the five of us ate in stony silence. Mother and Dad did not let on that they spoke fluent Japanese for fear they would be used as interpreters.

We wouldn't have worried had we known the truth. After our liberation we learned that the guard that accompanied us home that day was actually an American, born to Japanese parents who had immigrated to the United States. When the war broke out he was smuggled into Manila by submarine to act as a spy. I must say it was a shock to see him in an American Army uniform after the war. How he must have laughed inwardly when he remembered that day!

As summer turned to fall, Danny and I increasingly worried about the children's health. Alan was beset with constant colds and ear infections. It was nearly impossible to keep him incubated from all of the diseases that were so easily spread in our confined quarters. Finally, we made the difficult decision to send him to the Holy Ghost Convent outside the gates.

Holy Ghost was a boarding school for the children in camp under age 12. The children who went there received three meals a day and were given tender care by the nuns. Volunteer workers from the camp lived at the school, among them my sister Doreen. I was comforted that Alan would have one family member with him. Danny and I could only visit him once a week, but the visits confirmed our decision; he was well cared for and healthy.

Richard seemed to tolerate camp life better and attended the camp kindergarten a few hours a day. That fall, Richard and I were relocated from the Annex to the Main building. Our new room was larger than the one we had in the Annex and was a vast improvement, but it, too, was crowded and had its fair share of complaining women. I was "promoted" to Room Monitor; a thankless task that required me to arbitrate disputes among the residents.

As 1942 drew to a close, we internees became reconciled to our lot, but retained great faith in an ultimate victory by the Allies. Naturally, we spent a great deal of our time discussing the war and rumors of its progress were constantly making the rounds of camp. We soon learned that some rumors were based on a shred of truth, but most of them were made up by overactive imaginations. We suspected that there was a secret radio hidden in the camp and learned after the war that there had been one transmitter and receiver in camp, its whereabouts known only to five or six men. When these men received news of the war over the radio they made no mention of it until a corroborating story appeared in the *Manila Tribune* or some other external source. Often, the Executive Committee encouraged them to spread false rumors so that the Japanese would not suspect them of having an accurate source of information.

In an odd way, the *Tribune* also provided us with intelligence about the major battles taking place in the Pacific. The publishers would never admit the Japanese had lost any territory, but when they announced that the Japanese were bombing a certain island, it gave us knowledge of where the Allied forces were. We followed the events of the war in this way and were confident that MacArthur would make good on his promise to return. We just didn't know how long it was going to take.

By the spring of 1943, many Americans and British who had been allowed to live outside of Santo Tomas found life increasingly unbearable. They could no longer rely on old Filipino friends or servants for assistance, because the Japanese were making good on their threats to torture Filipinos who lent comfort and aide to Allied civilians. The food supply on the outside continued to be scarce, undependable and expensive. My parents were able to borrow money from some Swiss friends which enabled them to continue to lead a quiet and contained existence. Some of their Allied friends petitioned the Japanese for admission to Santo Tomas, since conditions in the camp were perceived to be better than on the outside. Mother and Dad decided to stick it out for as long as they could in the familiar comfort of their own home.

Santo Tomas began to fill with the civilians in Manila who had successfully petitioned to enter. At the same time, Allied civilians living on the outer islands were being rounded up by the Japanese and sent to the camp. Once again, overcrowding became a serious issue. In March, the Japanese announced a plan to build a new, bigger camp in Los Banos and relocate the camp there. Los Banos was a picturesque college town on a lake about 40 miles southeast of Manila. Most of us in camp were upset about the prospect of moving. Santo Tomas, for better or worse, was our home; we had built shanties, organized committees, grown vegetable gardens, and established routines.

After much negotiation between the Executive Committee and the commandant, they decided that the new camp in Los Banos would be opened, but only 800 prisoners from Santo Tomas would be transferred there. In May, the Executive Committee asked for volunteers to relocate to Los Banos. They specifically wanted men, mostly bachelors, who could build barracks in the new facility. As an accomplished carpenter, Danny was approached about moving. He was told that there was no guarantee that the boys and I would be able to follow him once the barracks were built. Ultimately, we both decided that a known hell was better than an unknown one so he declined the offer, but my brother, Jack, was recruited and accepted the transfer.

The transfer of the 800 prisoners immediately relieved the congestion. However, new arrivals continued to come in to camp every day and within weeks the population ballooned again to almost 3,700. The overcrowding became so bad that the Japanese finally relented and allowed the men to sleep in the shanties. Danny was thrilled to escape the confines of the men's barracks. Fresh air and his "home" made things a bit more bearable.

My living conditions in the women's building were close to intolerable. Sleep was hard to come by with so many children in one room; one crying infant seemed to spur on another all night long. Finally, the Japanese commandant withdrew his restriction on women sleeping in the shanties, and announced that married women could join their husbands. Paradoxically, he simultaneously issued an order prohibiting any further construction or expansion of the shanties. Unfortunately for Danny and me, our shanty was not large enough to accommodate the whole family, so Richard and I stayed in the dormitory until the restriction on construction was lifted.

Once the shanty issue was resolved the commandant began to address other matters. New rules seemed to emanate from his office on a daily basis and often times they seemed to be in contradiction. Some, for security or safety reasons, were closely adhered to. Others, such as the requirement to bow to all Japanese officers, were flouted on a routine basis. Three that remained constant were: no escapes, no alcohol and no fraternizing between the men and women.

The lack of alcohol presented no problem. Frankly, alcohol is consumed at a relatively young age in the tropics, probably due to the European influence going back so many years, so it was treated like any other beverage. I'm sure some people missed it, but Danny and I were fine without it.

We never thought of escape. In the first few days of internment, three people escaped and were re-captured. The Japanese marched them back into camp and tortured them in front of everyone. No one in their right mind would attempt to break out after witnessing that.

The lack of sexual activity wasn't too much of a hardship either. The inadequate diet and hard physical labor contributed to something close to indifference. By the time we women were allowed to sleep in the shanties, sex was the least of our priorities.

During the spring of 1943, the rumor mill in camp generated a tantalizing story: some number of internees would be repatriated to the United States in a prisoner exchange with Japan. We passed this story off as another example of wishful thinking but by mid-summer rumors of repatriation were rampant. In September word came that 150 civilians, 127 of them from Santo Tomas, were going to be released.

How the list of internees was selected has never been verified. The official explanation is that the U.S. State Department sent a list to Tokyo, naming the people to be repatriated. The two countries had agreed that any substitutions were to be filled by the Japanese Bureau of External Affairs in Manila. Some internees thought the Executive Committee also had a hand in determining the substitute list, so understandably there was much jockeying with its members to be one of the chosen few. Danny and I hoped that we would be selected, although we realized that Danny's British citizenship made it a remote possibility.

For my parents, however, fate and luck intervened. In late September they were surprised by a Japanese official knocking on their door. He politely entered the house, nervously sat down on the edge of their sofa and began to speak.

"Would you like to be a part of the prisoner exchange?" he asked.

Dad had heard the rumors about the prisoner exchange so he was prepared for the question. A friend had told him that the Japanese were having problems filling the quota of 150 prisoners because some internees, mostly those married to

Filipino girls, had declined the offer to leave Manila. Dad knew that the Japanese would want to "save face" and have the full complement of prisoners to exchange with the United States. So when Dad was offered this opportunity to return home he decided to up the ante.

"Yes," he replied, "we would like to leave but only if our two unmarried children, Doreen and Jack, can accompany us." Dad knew that asking for Tommy and I to be released, as well as our spouses and children, would have been perceived as too aggressive by the Japanese.

The official stared at Dad for a moment, but then nodded and granted the request. My parents quickly packed a few belongings and followed the official to his car. They were taken to Santo Tomas to spend the night before their departure the following day. My parents were grateful to have the opportunity to visit with Tommy and me and their beloved grandchildren to say good-bye.

On September 26 the citizens designated for repatriation were assembled in the courtyard in front of the Main building. We all came out to watch as they boarded the buses that would take them to their ship in the harbor. There was anger and resentment among some internees who had not been selected; charges of unfair procedures, favoritism, and bribery were heard all around. Still, the list was set at 150 and now that lucky group was assembled to say their good-byes. A few of the internees continued to plead their cases to the Executive Committee as the group boarded their buses.

I was thrilled that at least part of my family was escaping this captured existence. I knew that the rigors of life in Manila under Japanese occupation were taking a toll on my parents. Still, their departure was dreadfully hard for me. As I stood in the hot and crowded courtyard I could not find the right words of farewell. I shared an unusually close relationship with them; until I moved into the camp I had lived with or near them all my life. Our close proximity had allowed us to share life's smallest ups and downs.

I hugged them good-bye with tears and trepidation. They were leaving for a country that seemed a world away. I didn't know if they could survive the long voyage or, once there, where they would live. Worst of all, I didn't know if I would ever see them again. As their bus drove out of the main gate, I fell into Danny's arms and cried until there were no tears left.

Just as the furor over the repatriations settled down, we were faced with a monsoon season of epic proportions. More than thirty-seven inches of rain fell in a four week period. The wet weather wreaked havoc on the camp. It was impossible to keep our food stock dry so countless bags of rice and cornmeal were ruined. I couldn't protect our clothing from the dampness and humidity so a musty odor emanated from everything we wore. The worst consequence of the rain was the confinement it imposed on us. We had to spend time within the shelter of the buildings rather than in our shanty. Everyone in camp seemed to be in a foul mood; we shanty-dwellers hated squeezing into the crowded dorms, while the people in the dorms resented us making their crowded sleeping conditions more unbearable.

In January of 1944, our living conditions within Santo Tomas began to deteriorate drastically. The Japanese military took over "management" of the camp from the generally lenient Japanese diplomats. The new commandant came to us from a military POW camp, and he made it clear from the outset that we would be treated as enemies of the Japanese empire. The new officers treated us much more harshly than the civilian administrators and their punishing actions began almost immediately. Guards with fixed bayonets patrolled the grounds at all hours of the day and night. Surprise inspections became commonplace; the guards would burst into our shanty and rummage through our belongings without warning. They were stern and didn't seem to care about the unnerving affect their behavior had on Richard and Alan.

The new commandant's first directive was to shut down the "package line" and evict the vendors from camp. The severity of our loss of these two institutions cannot be overstated. The "package line" had provided us with a source for food, laundry and communication with friends and relatives on the outside. Its closure meant that we were cut off from the outside world.

With no vendors in camp we had to subsist solely on the rations provided in the general food line. Portions that were already meager were stretched beyond imagination. There was no meat to be found in the canteen line fare. Our two meals consisted of putrid fish served with mushy rice and overcooked talinum. Luckily, Danny and I had hoarded our food stocks from the Red Cross. We occasionally broke into our cans of meat when Richard and Alan seemed especially hungry, but mostly we survived on the rations provided at the canteen.

Our concerns over food became the topic of discussion at every meeting with the Executive Committee. We had seen a precipitous decline in the stipend we received from the Japanese each month. The Japanese paid the stipend to the Executive Committee in the currency they had established when they occupied the Philippines. Unfortunately, the Japanese flooded the country with their money, rendering it unstable from the onset. It was held in such low regard that we commonly referred to it as "Mickey Mouse" money.

Each of us was allocated thirty-five cents per day for food (equivalent to $3.64 in 2003 dollars) when the Japanese first took responsibility for feeding us in July

1942. But in mid-1943 the Japanese declared that the stipend not only had to cover the costs of our food, but also any costs associated with sanitation, utilities, construction, maintenance and sundry expenses. They stipulated that of the thirty-five cents allotted to us, only twenty-four cents was to be spent on food.

Prior to the war it was possible to provide nourishing, balanced meals for twenty-four cents, meals that included meat, fresh vegetables and fruit. But inflation had resulted in a downward spiral in the purchasing power of the Japanese currency and twenty-four cents no longer bought much. Prior to the eviction of the vendors we could supplement our stipend using our Filipino pesos[1] or American dollars. But when the supply of goods steadily grew worse, even the value of those currencies decreased. I paid 60 pesos for some shoes that had cost 9 pesos in 1941. It was the same for bread, eggs, peanuts, and goods such as Kleenex and cigarettes. As the war dragged on and inflation remained unchecked, the Japanese responded by printing more "Mickey Mouse" money, thus rendering it practically worthless by the end of 1943.

The stipend we received from the Japanese was subsequently increased to fifty-five cents per person, but the affect of spiraling inflation and the scarcity of food made this increase meaningless. By January, 1944, the twenty-four cents we had to spend on food was worth about eighteen cents and was lessening by the day.

The effects of our restricted diet began to appear within weeks. Some of the older and infirm internees began to suffer from complications of malnutrition: dry skin, listlessness and susceptibility to other diseases. The side-effects of our diet were apparent even to those of us who were young and healthy. I had an old pair of pants that had once been snug but now hung loosely on me. Since the beginning of our internment the Executive Committee had insisted that each internee be weighed and measured every month. By the spring of 1944 the men had lost an average of thirty-one pounds and the women averaged a loss of eighteen pounds since January 1942.

In June 1944 the commandant officially announced (although it was hardly news) that Santo Tomas was not being operated under the terms of the Geneva Convention. He declared that the military was not bound by any agreements enacted by the government in Tokyo. He insisted that the military could make their own laws and decisions regarding the operation of POW camps. He told us that the camp had officially been operating under these rules and regulations since February when the military had replaced civilian command. The Executive

---

1. Philippine pesos were worth approximately one-half of a United States penny at the time

Committee demanded to receive a copy of the new rules, but they were never provided with them.

The local Filipino population also began to suffer from the harsher military influence. The Filipinos had had an uneasy relationship with the Japanese throughout the war. The Japanese occupied the Philippines with the intent of freeing the Filipinos from their Westernized culture, and hoped to bring about a spirit of Asian "co-prosperity." But most Filipinos had great disdain for their occupiers.

The treatment that the Filipinos endured from the Japanese was the primary cause of the animosity. The Japanese military handled the local populace in a rough, and at times, humiliating manner. Women were not viewed with the respect they had become used to under American influence and resented their sudden plummet in status. The men did not fare much better. It was not unusual to see Japanese soldiers slapping or hitting a Filipino on the street for no apparent reason.

The troubled relationship between the two factions could be pinpointed on the food shortages and spiraling inflation. Most Filipinos were subsisting on whatever they could grow in their gardens and the few rations supplied by the Japanese. The Filipinos in Manila were required to show up for every public celebration of Japan's conquest; failure to attend resulted in confiscation of their food cards. The common phrase among the Filipinos was: "Our hearts are with the U.S. but our stomachs are with the Japanese."

Our worst fears about being captives of the Japanese seemed to be coming true. Up to this point we had relied on the terms of international agreements to hold them accountable, but now, as when they first entered the city in 1942, we worried about being tortured. We knew of their actions in other occupied territories and of what they were capable of when they did not fear reprisal from the outside world. We prayed for MacArthur to make good on his promise to return before we all perished.

Unbeknownst to us, plans were already underway for a major offensive in the Philippines. The Allied forces had begun a long, bloody counteroffensive in the Central and Southern Pacific Ocean, although it would be months before we inmates of Santo Tomas would hear credible accounts of the Allied victories. Major battles were led by MacArthur, heading the Army forces, and Admiral Chester Nimitz, leader of the naval fleet in the Pacific.

In July 1944 MacArthur and Nimitz traveled to Pearl Harbor to meet with President Roosevelt and discuss strategy for the eventual invasion of Japan. MacArthur's troops were poised in Sansapor, just 800 miles south of Mindanao, the southern tip of the Philippine Islands chain. Nimitz and his powerful naval fleet had battled their way through the Central Pacific island groups, moving through the Gilberts, Marshalls, Marianas, Guam, and finally, Tinian. By July they were only 1000 miles east of Luzon.

Nimitz and MacArthur, both with sizable egos, often argued over battle plans, and this decisive meeting with Roosevelt was no different. Nimitz wanted to establish anchorages and air bases on the central and southern islands of the Philippines, and head straight to Formosa, bypassing Luzon. MacArthur proposed an alternative plan, bearing straight for the Leyete Gulf in Mindanao and then up to Luzon. MacArthur desperately wanted to free the Philippines and he was not above using guilt to persuade Roosevelt. MacArthur argued that the inhabitants of the Philippines had depended on the United States for more than forty years for leadership and support. After the attack on Pearl Harbor, Roosevelt had pledged the full support of the United States in defending the Philippines from Japanese occupation. When the U.S. forces in the Philippines surrendered, Roosevelt again pledged to provide immediate relief and rescue.

For a variety of reasons, the most compelling being the war in Europe, Roosevelt had reneged on both pledges. Because of that, MacArthur maintained that the U.S. had a moral obligation to rescue the Philippines as soon as possible. He was a shrewd politician and was able to frame his argument in a way guaranteed to get Roosevelt's attention. MacArthur argued that if the U.S. ignored its commonwealth, it would not be well-received by the American public and could have negative political implications for Roosevelt in the upcoming presidential election.

MacArthur went on to assert that the Philippines had a major combat advantage over Formosa: its extensive guerilla network. As a result of the troubled relationship between the Filipinos and the Japanese, fierce guerilla forces had been formed immediately after the Japanese entered the Philippines. The guerilla networks operated primarily in the outlying provinces and had systematically bedeviled the Japanese during the course of the war. The guerillas numbered over 180,000 by mid-1944 and, emboldened by their successful attacks in remote locations, began to move back into Manila. Rumors of guerillas setting fire to piers and ships loaded with Japanese supplies in Manila harbor had already reached MacArthur.

Finally, in an argument intended to goad Nimitz, MacArthur stressed that the most logical base of operations for the Navy was Luzon. Manila Bay was the only port large enough to accommodate the large fleet necessary for the planned invasion of the Japanese mainland. Ultimately, either from guilt, persuasion, or both,

Roosevelt agreed with MacArthur that the Philippines, primarily Luzon, should be the main objective of the Allied forces. MacArthur was buoyed by the meeting and the prospect of liberating his captured troops and civilian friends.

The Japanese high command in Tokyo had correctly surmised that the Allies would converge in the Philippines. Once the backwater of the war, the Philippines took on unprecedented importance to the Japanese and became a pivotal base of operations. Manila harbor was midway between Tokyo and the Japanese-occupied Indies, and was the site of supply exchanges for their fleet. The fleet south of the archipelago received arms and ammunition sent from Tokyo while the fleet north of the Philippines, the fleet that would be primary in the defense of Japan, received their fuel supplies from the Indies. The generals knew that if the Allied forces recaptured the Philippines, the supplies lines would be cut off and the war would be lost.

The Japanese generals' desire to bolster their chances for victory caused them to transfer their most talented general, Tomoyuki Yamashita, from Vietnam to the Philippines. When Yamashita arrived in Manila he was horrified to see the condition and training of his soldiers; they were lazy and out of shape. Yamashita knew that a major conflict was in the offing and made immediate changes to the daily routine and discipline of the men under his command. If the Allies launched a major assault on the Philippines, he was going to be sure that they were in top fighting condition.

In Tokyo, the reports of U.S. victories in the Central and Southern Pacific Ocean negatively affected the spirits of the military and citizenry. In an effort to boost morale, officers in the field were encouraged to exaggerate their accomplishments: the number of enemy planes shot down, men killed, or ships sunk. The top military officers were anxious about the direction the war was taking and wanted to report only good news to the Emperor. To their detriment, the Japanese generals began to believe the inflated reports and gained misplaced confidence with each new account. In Manila, Yamashita's biggest problem was not his ill-trained men but his belief in the propaganda about the decimation of the Allied forces. He was confident that he could repel any attack from MacArthur and Nimitz.

The strutting officers in Santo Tomas reflected Yamashita's confidence. Their behavior, coupled with our lack of nutritious food, made our situation seem desperate. Many of us broke out in skin rashes and boils from the stress. We were filled with apprehension about the future and our hopes for rescue grew dimmer.

3

The Diary

In August 1944 we received our last, and most vicious, commandant, Colonel Hayashi. We all concluded that Hayashi, along with his right hand man, Lieutenant Abiko, were the most inhumane and cruel officers we encountered in Santo Tomas. Arbitrary and brutal, they meted out punishment for the most minor of infractions. Men were arrested and put in the camp jail for failing to bow properly to the Japanese guards. A friend of ours walked too near the outside wall one day. His punishment was to stand still for more than seven hours; if he shifted his weight or bent his knees the Japanese guards beat his legs with bamboo poles.

Hayashi was unrelenting in his denial of our requests for additional rations, despite the obvious and alarming affects of malnutrition on many of us. In his first thirty days in camp, he cut our rice ration by twenty-five percent, to just three hundred grams per person. This is equivalent to approximately 1,000 calories per day. The Executive Committee asked Hayashi for permission to dip into the camp stocks, long held in reserve for just such a decrease in rations. Hayashi's response was that the stocks were being held in Japanese custody in a secret location which could not be revealed to us. He suggested that the prisoners who worked in the gardens plant more vegetables; a suggestion made ludicrous by the obvious weakened condition of the workers.

The rumor-mill in camp had historically provided us with overly optimistic conjectures. Danny and I both observed that the rumors' tone changed as our food grew scarcer and the guards became crueler. The main topic of most rumors was our perceived abandonment by the United States. It became more difficult for us to remain optimistic and a dark gloominess fell over the camp.

As the summer dragged on each passing day seemed to last a year. Once we had completed our daily chores we had little to keep ourselves occupied. Most of us didn't feel up to much in the way of physical activity. Games as sedentary as bridge seemed not worth the effort it took to sit for hours at a time. One by one, the men abandoned their sports teams when not enough people could be mustered to field a squad.

We all adopted the rather ridiculous past-time of reading through cook books, drooling over the pictures of food. I exchanged recipes with some of my friends; the more exotic the dish, the better. At one point I made out menus for an entire year, planning for the day when we would be released and I could get the proper ingredients.

Danny occupied himself with studying the weather. He had always been interested in weather and had purchased a barometer from a camp vendor shortly after he entered Santo Tomas. The barometer was his most prized possession, and he spent hours predicting the weather with his friend, Les Fennel. Les had been a meteorologist with the Pan American Airways office in Manila. Les and the other Pan Am employees had been interned in Santo Tomas with us.

One pastime that caught on with many of us in camp was writing in a diary or journal. Memoir writing had been a popular pastime prior to the war, and was an activity we could do that didn't sap our energy. People began keeping diaries for a variety of reasons. Some wanted to document the experience for themselves or family members; others did it as a way to combat boredom. Even the Executive Committee joined in, naming a former journalist, A.V.H. Hartendorp, as the official camp historian to diary the events in the camp and the actions of the Japanese.

We knew that keeping a diary of any sort was hazardous. The Japanese were suspicious of anything we wrote and therefore forbade any communication except letters, which they reserved the right to censor. Internees who were caught with written material that was critical of the Japanese were taken to Fort Santiago, a military post in Manila, where they were kept in the 16th century dungeons and tortured, in most cases, to death.

I longed to start a diary for my parents as a way to journal what we were experiencing in the camp. I thought if I could write an entry each day it would help me believe that I was actually talking with them. My biggest concern was how I could hide the diary from the Japanese guards. I needed to find a place that would not be obvious to them during one of the many surprise searches they made of the shanty. I devised what I considered a brilliant plan: each day I could roll the diary up in the mosquito netting before it was tossed up on the roof. I knew that there was some danger in this, but decided it was a risk worth taking.

So these many years later I have the following record of exactly what happened to Danny, Richard, Alan and me for the remainder of the war. Here, as written sixty years ago, is our story of pain, endurance and the faith needed to survive a hell on Earth.

July 26, 1944

My dear Mother:

I am starting to do now what I intended to do last year after you left—write a sort of diary-letter that I can send on to you as soon as the war is over. In that way you can see for yourself just what kind of a time we've had. However, like most good intentions, this one did not come into effect. So many things happened to interfere but now I have determined to do my best to write a little every day. We are going through rather a bad time just now. Sometimes I wonder if we will come out of it alive, and whether we shall ever see you again. Thank God you are out of it all! One does feel, though, that it would be rather unkind of Providence to snuff us out at this late date when we've gone through so much already.

Ten months since you left! It doesn't seem possible. I wonder so often where you are, what you are doing—if you are well and happy.

Life was very dull after you left, after the tumult and the shouting had died down. But not for long. You know, we have the saying here "Never a dull moment in Santo Tomas"—and how true that has been.

We had a dreadful rainy season, to begin with. It went on until February. You know, rain makes life so much more difficult in here. The first thing that happened to us was that the laundry arrangement you made for us didn't last long. In October, the woman sent word that she had to have more money. I've been doing all the washing ever since and feel I am now a qualified *lavendera*. Talk about "tattle-tale grey", though! Soap is absolutely unobtainable apart from a very small ration which we are given from time to time. When I come to the end of my stock, I shall simply have to do as some of my friends are already doing—do without.

On a dreary rainy afternoon towards the end of October, the quiet was broken by the sound of a truck coming down the road—grim specter of an ambulance from San Lazaro hospital. It had come to take out poor Bill Waldo, suddenly stricken with polio. The whole camp was gloomy over this—the terror that dread disease strikes to every heart!

Well, we said, we've been lucky. Nearly two years without an epidemic. But, just as troubles never come singly, so diseases follow rapidly. A case of measles was discovered in the Children's Hospital. It was a child who had just come from the outside. He was taken to the hospital immediately but the infection had spread and we have had as pretty an epidemic of measles as you could wish for. Oh, but not only measles came to visit us. Whooping cough, chicken pox and bacillary dysentery began attacking the camp. The dormitory was turned into an isolation hospital and is still being used for that purpose. But of this, more later as I will attempt to keep some sort of order.

In November, great excitement reigned as the "Teia Maru" [a Japanese supply ship] arrived in port carrying the Red Cross packages intended for us. Volunteers went down to unload our precious relief supplies which were then stored in a downtown bodega. We had to wait, of course, for gracious permission from the Japanese before they could come into camp.

Meanwhile, it rained. And rained. On November 21st the barometer started falling steadily. It blew harder towards evening and the camp weatherman predicted that the typhoon would probably hit Manila that evening. He wanted the Committee to warn people over the loud speaker so that the shanty sleepers could take some sort of precautions. But the Committee refused on the grounds that a panic might ensue. It was too bad that they took this stand because the typhoon did arrive about midnight. It was one of the worst ones we've ever had, too. One of the good old-fashioned varieties. I was so thankful that you were not here! The force of the wind was such that the windows in the Main building shook with nerve-racking intensity. All night long fathers came in with children (those that slept in the shanties).

In the morning we were scared to see what damage had been wrought. How many shanties had been wrecked? To my joy, I could see that our shanty was still standing! The camp presented such a scene of desolation. Trees down—one fell on the Playhouse causing considerable damage. Tommy's shanty was completely wrecked. He moved into ours and slept there for several weeks until he could rebuild.

I was awfully worried about Alan and was relieved when I heard Mr. Duggleby had waded all the way over to Holy Ghost and brought back the news they were all fine over there.

After three days, the rain finally stopped, and the flooding finally subsided, leaving havoc and devastation in its wake. Everything in the shanty was wet and dirty, but as I said before, we were much luckier than most.

Well, things finally got straightened out. We all caught up with washing and cleaning. Back to normal again with the next excitement on the list—the arrival in camp of the relief supplies. We had heard all sorts of rumors to the effect that they had been under water in the outside warehouses so you can imagine our relief when they arrived intact. They were not given out immediately as they had to be inspected first.

The Japanese inspection party arrived finally and aroused the camp to fever pitch. Every case was taken out and put in the roadway, between the Main Building and the Commandant's office. The first case was uncrated and to our horror, *every can* had been opened! We were having hysterics watching, seeing all that precious food wasted. Oh, Mother, only a hungry internee can feel what we did then, seeing *Klim* [powdered milk] stirred with a bayonet! However, they soon tired of this "sport"!

Distribution of the kits started that afternoon. Every internee received a complete kit containing four boxes of food—minus the cigarettes. What had apparently started the idea of inspection was that the packages of Old Gold cigarettes bore a slogan for Victory on the wrapping and that annoyed the Japanese. All the cigarettes were removed. The Old Golds were taken out of the packages and given out loose to the people in the outside institutions. We were given the other brands later—forty-two packs per person.

But the comfort kits! Oh, Mother, I truly believe that they have literally saved our lives! They contained so much good food. We have conserved ours and still have a good supply to tide us over this present dreadful period. To see chocolate again and cheese and prunes!!

As for the medical supplies, well, they *have* saved our lives and helped so many of us. The vitamin pills and serum have kept most people going.

The camp had a real problem to decide on an equitable distribution of the clothing. There was enough to go around for the women but so little for the men. Finally they worked out a "points" system, similar to the clothing ration we had last year. Every woman received a play-suit (shorts, blouse and skirt) either printed cotton or plain sateen in different colors, a pair of panties, shoes, socks, toothbrush, tooth powder, comb, toilet soap, laundry soap, shoelaces, handkerchief, sewing kit, and a seer-sucker nightgown.

We were all delighted to get them. Later distribution based on points gave us our choice of another pair of shoes or cold cream—items which were not in sufficient quantity to go around.

The children got underwear, shirts and trousers, powder, pajamas, shoes and socks. Unfortunately, there were no shoes for children between six and twelve. Poor Richard didn't get any (and he needs them so badly) but Alan got two pairs.

July 28, 1944

Dear Mother:

I find it hard to sit down and write for any particular length of time, so I am afraid this will be a rather piecemeal account. The men fared rather badly on the relief supplies as there was not enough of any one item to go around. There was a storm of controversy over the shoes question. Every man needed a pair of shoes and the question of making a fair distribution was very difficult. The "powers that be" [the Executive Committee] finally sent out a questionnaire asking all men to answer honestly; if a man had a pair of shoes which could be repaired, he would be given two sets of soles and heels (shoe repair kits had been included in the supplies) and thus release a pair of new shoes to the man who had no old ones worth repairing. This seemed to work out satisfactorily.

Not only were the contents of the cases very welcome, but the empty cases themselves filled a real need. Every scrap of lumber and every nail were carefully saved and have been used in repair work.

Scarcely had the excitement of the relief supplies died down, when a fresh outburst took place. This was in early December, the long-awaited transfer to Los Banos of the wives and sweethearts of the men up there building the new camp. The women nearly went crazy! That was one order given out which really pleased everyone. We were so tired of having the women make up petitions to the Commandant that we were as glad to see them go as they were. They left in the middle of the night as the loudspeaker blared "Wedding March" and a final burst of "It Will Be a Hot Time in the Old Town Tonight" as the trucks drove off!

Before we knew it, Christmas was upon us again. A very good day it was, too, although not to be compared with the one of the year before. We did miss you so much, Mother and Dad! Wondered all day where you were spending Christmas.

The camp had secured permission for a shipment of toys to be purchased which parents in turn were allowed to buy—standing in line, of course! We could get two toys for every child, which was not too bad. And we could buy more from the vendors—at a price! We got Alan a truck and a stocking filled with small toys. Danny made him a huge wooden truck and I made him a scrapbook. For Richard I got two pairs of trousers made, two shirts, books, etc.

Of course we were all up at the crack of dawn on Christmas Day. Richard was so excited over his stocking! When we got down to the shanty, Danny had arranged his presents under the "tree" (the same bush which we used last year) and he was so pleased with everything. We had breakfast at the restaurant and then I went to church in the garden.

Alan arrived from Holy Ghost around ten—very thrilled with his bus ride. We had such a happy day with him. The Hunter's had an eggnog party that morning and I took Alan—he behaved so well.

After lunch we had the party for the children on the front lawn. Santa Claus came in through the gate and distributed the gifts. Then we all had ice cream and cake. Alan was so tired when he left!

New Year's Eve came and went in a blaze of glory. It was really a very wet occasion. Goodness knows where the rum came from but it certainly flowed like water. We had a grand stage show, an old-fashioned pantomime, of "Cinderella". It started late, due to a quick shower, and was very long so the plaza wasn't clear until about ten-thirty. Quite an occasion, you see.

On January 2nd, the Davao internees [Davao is a city on the island of Mindanao] arrived late in the evening. They were certainly a ragged, dirty set of people. They had been ten days in the hold of a rat-infested ship, packed in like sardines—men, women and children. They were so thankful to be here as Santo Tomas seemed a veritable Paradise to them.

Santo Tomas a Paradise! Yes, looking back it was indeed. We had the cold stores, canteen, market, package line, vendor's stalls, and restaurants. This was our "prison camp" in January, 1944. Looking back over the past seven months, I can see that our decline has matched the rising tide of the Allies' success in the Pacific.

July 30, 1944

Our troubles really seemed to begin with the change in Commandants. In December, Mr. Kudaki and Mr. Kuroda left. Our new Commandant was Mr. Kato, a repatriate from England. In December, incidentally, the rumors of repatriation for the British were so hot that people actually offered to buy up their comfort kits! I think something must have been in the air for the British Committee asked us to state where we would like to go. This all seems so long ago!

The first thing Mr. Kato did was to order the closing of the vendors and the restaurants. He had socialistic ideas and was therefore against any private enterprise. The closing of the restaurants was rather a blow to us as Danny was still working at John Hunter's restaurant and we were eating well. However, what could be done about it? Nothing!

The next step was a change over in market. The Filipinos were no longer allowed to come in but the produce was still permitted in with the internees in charge of the selling. The canteen buyers were no longer allowed to go out. So the canteen has now dwindled to practically nothing. No meat came in to the cold stores.

Most serious of all, however, was the change in our daily line fare. The Committee had been asking for an increase in our daily allowance so as to enable us to buy more. Due to inflation, the purchasing power of the peso was falling rapidly. You will remember that our first allowance was 35 pesos per day which covered not only food but light, gas, water and medical supplies. This was increased to

1.10 pesos with about 97 pesos being spent on food. When pressed for an increase to 1.50 pesos per day, the Japanese unexpectedly took matters into their own hands and decided to treat this camp exactly as a War Prisoner's Camp. They announced that instead of giving us money, they would supply us with food. They said they would supply us with so many grams per head of rice, corn, coconuts and fish. Also, vegetables when they are available. Children were to be on a half-ration. Mr. Carroll from the Committee assured us that the children had always and would continue to have first consideration. He also went on to say that the camp would be able to buy supplementary foods with Red Cross funds, private loans, etc.

Now, at this time the package line was still open so people laughed at the "rice and fish" idea. We could still buy all we wanted at the market. I must say the fish was a bit of a shock. Mother, do you remember telling Nicasio [the cook] to buy five cents worth of fish for the cats, and how he said he was ashamed to because the other cooks thought he was going to eat it? Well, that is the kind of fish we were given! A special "fish detail" was formed for the purpose of cleaning the fish and on the three days a week when fish came in, the place smelled like Quiaps Market on a bad day!

Early in February the Japanese provided us with a new sensation by announcing the closing down of Holy Ghost and Sulphur Springs. When we protested (it becomes a habit) on the grounds of over-crowding, the Japs finally gave their permission for women to sleep in the shanties. This was a concession we had been asking for and one which we scarcely thought we would get. A quarter of the camp's population is now housed in shanties. Danny and Richard were both sleeping in the shanty by this time but I didn't move down as we had no room for four. We had started an extension but the "new order" had stopped the entry of nipa into the camp so we were stuck. They went further and forbade any alterations at all to be made. This is so like their inconsistency. They allowed families to sleep in shanties and then stopped them from enlarging or repairing!

We were very pleased to have Alan back with us. We intended to bring him back before Christmas but the measles and whooping cough epidemic made me change my mind. By February, however, everyone said "bombing in March" so we thought it a good plan to have him back.

July 31, 1944

Well, early in February Alan was returned to us. We found him so improved and so much easier to take care of. Holy Ghost had made him very independent. He's been such a joy to us ever since.

About this time Danny was laid up with an infected foot. It started from a mere scratch but got so bad he was forced to lie up for a while. This made rather a lot of trouble for me as I had to stand in two food lines, three times a day. However, after about two weeks he was up again but only for a few days. His foot got so much sorer that he had to go back to bed for four weeks. It must have been very much the same trouble as Dad had. You can imagine the bad time we had! Danny had rather a bad reaction from the sulpha and felt very miserable.

I'm sorry I can't remember the date of the next "bombshell" as it would be interesting. Please remember that I am not attempting to write a detailed or accurate history of the camp—I leave that to more experienced hands.

Well, this occurred sometime in February: the Japanese announced one evening that they wanted every internee to be lined up outside his room the following morning at eight o'clock as they were going to take Roll Call. Now, you may remember that we used to have roll call every evening at nine o'clock but this was done by the internee monitors. Accordingly, we lined up, children and all and by nine-thirty the count was over. Incidentally, they played a recording at six-thirty in order to awaken everyone, and breakfast was served only from six-thirty to seven-thirty. It seemed funny to be up and dressed in pitch darkness. Well, after two days of this the Japanese apparently got tired of counting noses for they delegated that duty back to the monitors. We still had to line up every morning at eight and every evening at seven, however. The Japs contented themselves with paying us surprise visits. We very soon got used to this, though, and roll call is now so much a party of our routine that we would feel lost without it. In fact, for those who live in the shanties it is quite a social gathering as it is at that time that we see all our friends.

We had one bad experience, though. One Sunday morning we were informed that the Japanese were going to take a special roll call at twelve noon. We lined up in the hot sun and were there until two-fifteen! Then at four o'clock we had to line up again until five-fifteen. I still don't know why, but they had guards all over the place and they counted very carefully. There was a rumor that someone had gone over the wall but we never knew the true story.

In early March Richard came down with the measles but it was quite a light case. He was in the Isolation Hospital ten days. Alan went in a week later but had a much worse case. The ward was crowded with crying children, it was dark, of course, and very hot and *smelled,* that particular measles smell! Alan had ear complications twice but after that they were both fine.

Things were gradually getting tighter at this time. We now had ration cards for the market and were limited in our purchases. Every internee was allowed to buy an egg a day and we were allowed one loaf of bread a day for the four of us. What luxury! We didn't have that long. They stopped the bread first and the eggs gradually lessened until it was an egg a week! At this time we have not been able to buy any eggs for nearly a month. The last we paid for them was 2.60 pesos per egg.

It was in March or April that a new order was put into effect—no more cooking in the shanties! You can imagine what a blow this was. We were all forced to carry our stoves and cooking apparatus out in the open. It was such a nuisance but people took it well and there was much exchanging of "recipes". As a substitute for bread, most of us were making hot cakes of mush, flour and coconut milk. They were good, too. Now I look back on them longingly. After a few days we were allowed to cook in groups just outside our shanties. Then at last we were given permission to cook inside again.

We were now under military administration and Mr. Kato was replaced by a colonel. We were told the night before that he would make an inspection of the camp and that we must show proper respect by bowing. Well, the Colonel and about twenty officers passed our shanty, stopped and spoke to us, asked what we were cooking. He really seemed to take an interest in the camp. He was always summoning us to the Plaza and giving us pep talks!

Incidentally, we had quite amusing experiences with the Colonel. He was very fond of walking around the camp (Snoopy Sam we called him) and he very often passed our shanty. The first time he passed the children both called out to him so he stopped and spoke to them. I was having silent hysterics because Alan kept saying, "Mummy, I *like* this Japanese guy!" Fortunately, I don't think he got the meaning of the word "guy" but the officer with him did because he laughed like anything! The good Colonel came again the next day with candy for the children and we asked him to sit down. He did for a few minutes. Painful conversation of course! After that he came often. Once the children were not here and he said to me, "Send for them". Another time he took Alan off with him. I got a bit worried so I sent Richard after him. There was Master Alan sitting in the office consuming buttered toast!

Incidentally, the Japs softened a bit and allowed shanty repairs to go on. So, as we were allowed to finish our extension, Alan and I moved down. By making a double-decker bed, we have plenty of room and I like it so much better. It makes life simpler and is very pleasant in the evenings not to have to rush upstairs.

I think that I have brought things fairly well up to date in a very general way and can go on and give a day-by-day report. I've probably forgotten lots of things but will put them in as I remember them.

Now, frankly, we are a hungry camp. In fact, damned hungry. The package line closed in February. That was the worst thing we had to put up with in most people's opinion. Personally, I miss peanut butter, our last link with the protein world. Oh, yes, no more peanuts could be bought in Manila.

Last month the Japs stopped bringing in corn. Our daily diet is now as follows: Breakfast, rice mush and coconut milk, a slice of camp-made rice bread (heavy, tough, tasteless—unbelievably delicious when spread with hunger sauce!). For lunch, rice and soup, very thin. For dinner, rice and gravy. We get bananas rarely now. The gravy is made from our camp stock of canned meats which we have been saving for an emergency. This is regarded as so serious a time that we have to open them. The children fare a little better, as we get eggs occasionally. The fish comes in irregularly and is never enough so that all we can have with it is fish gravy.

Some time ago a complete reorganization of the Central Kitchen took place. The line food became suddenly important to the Big Shots [Executive Committee] who had never had to eat off the line before. It was discovered that the present crew was stealing food right and left. John Hunter was made chief cook with three crews under him. Danny heads one of these crews. Everyone now has to eat from the line or starve. Of course, many people are using canned goods as well but we all feel that an even worse emergency may threaten us. We can buy so little in the market so everyone is hungry.

We have no sugar ration at all and no coffee or cigarettes. The children are still getting a pudding once in a while but this is made from reserve stock. Of course, sugar and cigarettes come in sub-rosa—at a price. I understand sugar is 20.00 peso per kilo outside. The other day we bought a kilo for 190.00 pesos. We sold two cans of jam and bought sugar instead. Inflation, of course!

I see that I have made no mention of a change in camp management. The Commandant decided we didn't need a large Committee; moreover, he objected to the title of Executive Committee as implying too much power. So he appointed the Internee Committee. A group of internees conversant with the Geneva Conference were trying to get the Japs to recognize it. They went so far as to allow us to elect three Internee Agents. These Agents, working with the Committee, protested about the food but to no avail. The answer is always the same: There is no food and we are fed as well as the army. Moreover, word came from military headquarters that they had no intention of recognizing the Geneva Conference.

August 1, 1944

Dear Mother and Dad,

Our little Richard was seven today. His third birthday since the war started, his third and last, I hope. At any rate, on the strength of all the good new news, we have been promising him all sorts of things for *next* August! At any rate, he has had a very happy day of it. Danny made him a sailboat (boats are all the rage—they sail them in mud puddles). And we found an old penknife for him. I made him an apron with C.K. (Central Kitchen) on it—just like Daddy's—and a couple of arm bands. We had such beautiful weather and so unusual for August. I made him a chocolate cake. You would laugh if you knew what I put into it and what I didn't. And we had ice cream! This last was a complete surprise to him and the way we managed it was this: we have become quite friendly with one of the Episcopal padres from Davao, Raymond Abbott. He works at the Isolation Hospital and has access to an ice box (sh!). We had one tin of condensed milk and this plus a couple of mangoes and some gulamen [native gelatin] made lovely ice cream. Of course, we couldn't begin to have a party but Richard's friend, Robert, came over and had supper with us. So I think Richard will always have pleasant enough memories of his seventh birthday.

However, the day was spoiled for us grown-ups by the announcement which we have just listened to. Of course, it was made in the most dramatic manner by one of our Committeemen. He started off by saying this was the worst announcement the Committee had ever had to make. It was short and to the point. The Committee had been advised that all internees would have to turn into the Bank of Taiwan all our money. This, the order says, is for our own good because 1) it will save us from robbery, 2) will gather interest (loud laughter), and, finally, 3) will prevent us from spending it for unnecessary things. We will be allowed to draw 50.00 pesos per month. He went on the say that the Committee will hold further discussions with the Commandant tomorrow and that we would be kept advised.

Well, they have taken from us so much already that a little more won't hurt us.

August 2, 1944

Dear Mother and Dad,

Well, no chance of improving the money situation and everyone has gone mad today; the "haves" buying anything at the most fantastic prices and the "have-nots" selling in order to get enough money to put into the bank. The

Committee announced that anyone with surplus cash could put it into a camp pool so that buying extra food may continue. These loans would be backed with Red Cross receipts.

I was so thrilled today to receive your letter written last February. We had just received one from Mrs. Watson in January saying she had heard from you, and I was saying how much I wished we could hear from you when Lolita came over with your letter. So, you are in Los Angeles! I would give a great deal to have received a 'real' letter as I know you must have volumes to write. However, we are so thankful to know where you are and that you are well. Everyone is so pleased to hear news of you. Your letter from Goa, written in October, arrived in June! I was so pleased and excited—just to see your handwriting again was enough for me. You say you are homesick for us! What wouldn't I give to see you again? But I am so thankful that you have missed all this!

The camp is really completely isolated now, but we do get some news. The Japs stopped the paper coming in June and that was a real blow. However, just before it stopped we were able to read about the opening of the second front in Europe and that sent us wild with joy. We have just heard of Hitler's death—is it true or not? You know it's funny, but we are all afraid to believe anything. We *know* the end is approaching but we can't visualize this life ever coming to an end. God grant it may end soon.

Since April we have had practice air raids off and on with blackout regulations in force. The Japanese have built machine gun nests at the front and back gates. They evidently expect something!

Last month they suddenly rounded up all the missionaries, nuns and padres and brought them into the Gym, which had been cleared of occupants. We were not allowed to see or speak to them. The next day they were all shipped off to Los Banos.

August 4, 1944

Thirty years ago today since the "War to End All Wars" began. What a farce!

The Medical Council is very worried over the health of the camp since we began our rice diet. Most concerned are the three army doctors who were brought here from Cabanatuan some time ago. They have seen first hand the affects of a starchy diet and have written a very strong letter to the Commandant saying that they will not be held responsible. So many people are suffering from beriberi and pellagra. Others are jut collapsing. Honestly, Mother, we are hungry all the time. Even the children clamor for more food constantly. We can buy scarcely anything in the market. A handful of rice with a little gravy over it is not very much.

And yet, we keep going! We wash and iron, air beds and sweep much as usual. Our rice is served on a nice china plate, and we still sit at a table with a cloth on it and flowers! They *won't* get us down!

In March the Japs demanded that we turn into them all our electric irons, clocks, hot plates, etc. For a while we had to iron with charcoal, and then they turned back a few irons. We now have a special ironing room where we may iron once a week.

Richard has had bacillary dysentery and Alan has had three attacks of it. Fortunately, this is a mild type, nothing like that dreadful disease that attacked Richard three years ago. But they both have suffered from fevers and diarrhea.

We hear that Quezon is dead [Quezon died on August 1 of tuberculosis]. If this is true, what a pity he did not live to see the Philippines retaken. They say the Filipinos on the outside are starving. I don't think they can have any love for their conquerors. Co-prosperity does not appeal to them any more than it does to us!

August 14, 1944

As I said previously, we are awakened every morning at six-thirty by a record, the choice of which is sometimes most amusing and apt. For the news of the invasion of France, they played "It's a Hap-hap-happy Day", with a bar or two of "Over There" in between. They really like us to wake up smiling!

So far the rainy season is not too bad. I only hope we don't have another flood. The rain is hard on the children, being cooped up in the shanty, and it is hard on the laundry. However, a few bright days in between bouts dries everything out so we can't complain.

Richard started school in June and is now in second grade. He is doing fairly well although they only have an hour and a half due to lack of books and equipment. He is a strange mixture of extreme good and bad. He can be so obstinate and disobedient that we are really at a loss to cope with him. Of course, this life does not overly help problems of discipline. On the other hand, he is so good with Alan and can be sweet and helpful. I think he will turn out all right but how I long to get him into a really good school and away from the majority of the untrained *brats* around here!

Master William Alan Watson is of course still at the cute stage and is really irresistible. He never stops talking, eats more than any child I ever saw, and is full of vitality. He is as cheeky as possible but is so funny that he can get away with it.

He rules his slave, Richard, with a rod of iron and Danny is just pulp in his hands. He is extremely selfish and jealous! Can't bear to have me show Richard any affection and it has taken me a long time to convince him the R. is just as much our boy as he is. But he is a darling. I'm so sorry that you can't see him. And when I think that his other Grannie has never seen him I could weep! I trust you have given her good accounts of both boys.

Yesterday we were informed that our new Commandant was arriving. We seem to change Commandants as often as France used to change governments. Everyone says that no one wants to be in charge when the end comes. Our "friend", the Colonel, was replaced by a civilian, Mr. Onazaki, some time ago and now he in turn is replaced by another army man, Colonel Hayashi. Things always seem to get worse with each change! Alan adores the Japanese and has no fear of them at all. He is always running after the soldiers and holding hands with them! Well, I am glad that he feels none of the antipathy towards them that we do. He won't remember any of this and I hope Richard will remember only the pleasant parts of it.

Our entertainments are now few and far between. We had an excellent minstrel show several months ago. A quartet composed of four excellent singers from Davao sang a very clever and amusing piece about the camp. We can still laugh at ourselves, you see. There was one bit about our going to the line three times a day and getting nothing to eat. This annoyed the Japs so that they made Dave Harvey apologize! Since then we have had no more shows. We have a movie twice a month but usually very poor ones. The best we ever had was "Dumbo" which was shown last Christmas. People flock to the Plaza, of course, because it is still a movie, no matter how poor and we are starved for entertainment.

August 15, 1944

Today is Dad's birthday. Many happy returns! When I told the children this morning, Alan immediately said that he wanted to go to Grandpa's birthday party!

This morning we were told a high official would visit the camp—they often come to inspect the "zoo". Shortly after this announcement, about twenty soldiers came trotting along with tin hats and fixed bayonets, each with a branch of hibiscus fastened onto his back. I must say they looked rather sheepish, especially as the children all cheered them! I suppose they were to impress the visiting firemen with their alertness. As one of our neighbors wittily remarked, "Don't they know that only God can make a tree?" We never saw any sign of the visitors so wonder if they were only practicing.

One can't help but think that perhaps the end is really approaching. Certainly the Japs themselves seem to expect it. After all, the Commandant himself is seen digging an air-raid shelter! Yesterday the hospital was told to prepare forty "leg-amputation blocks". Sounds gruesome! The bombings of Davao seem true enough and Roosevelt is supposed to have said that the attack on the Philippines has begun. I don't suppose it will be particularly pleasant for us here when they start on Manila. Let's hope it will be brief. I wonder if this notebook will last out! I wonder, too, if I will finish it or if you will ever receive it. Will we perhaps sit and read it together? Oh, Mother, I do hope we will come through safely. This period of waiting is so hard to endure. We count for so little actually, but so much to ourselves!

August 21, 1944

The weeks wear by! Still waiting for that sweetest of music, the wail of the sirens followed by the drone of planes and then—boom! Who would have thought that we would sit and pray for those sounds! Last night there was quite a spiel over the radio about air-raid procedures. For the first time in the history of the camp, they came right out and openly said that "as the war was now intensified, Manila was in danger of being bombed." Usually they have skirted around and said "if something happens". The Japs are feverishly constructing more shelters—for themselves, of course. Davao bombings continue so perhaps we may be out soon.

Every Saturday afternoon they have been having little programs for the kiddies in the Playhouse, ending up with singing. Last Saturday we had a Scottish program and Richard was in the chorus and had such fun practicing. Alan's version of Loch Lomond: "you take the high *rope* and I'll take the low rope and I'll be in the States before you!" Richard and the chorus did very well. All the parents enjoyed it very much.

The Japs have been practicing anti-aircraft firing all afternoon. Too bad it isn't the real thing. I am feeling bitter tonight because, as usual, we are hungry. We had unusually poor gravy tonight and the rice was burned and lumpy. The children had rice and a small portion of scrambled eggs for their supper. That, with a glass of calamansi juice, is all we've had. Not even a banana. When I want to get a meal by proxy I study the recipe books and think about the meals we will have someday. This is a form of self-torture which I do not recommend. When I think of my poor children with never a cookie or piece of candy—to say nothing of all the good nourishing food which we are doing without—I feel nothing but the sternest hatred for the Japanese. They are actually supplying us with nothing but rice and coconuts at this time. Whatever vegetables we have we buy ourselves.

Occasionally they send in some radishes. The fish is never enough to go around (so it goes to the children and the hospital) and when, on rare occasions, they send in meat it is only enough to make into a gravy.

How long, oh Lord, how long?

August 23, 1944

It's just eleven months since you left!

We had a practice blackout last night and are still "under alert" so that I suppose we will be blacked out again tonight. Anti-aircraft practice has continued throughout the day. I feel a little better tonight as we had fried rice for supper which is rather more filling than rice and gravy.

So far we are having a very mild rainy season. I hope it will continue to be mild as we do not want a repetition of last year.

August 27, 1944

Still under alert and blacked out again tonight. Yesterday we got the story that the American flag is flying in Davao. It could be true, but is it? We are all just waiting. There is a dream-like quality about these days as though each were a page of a book numbered and nearing the end. It must be coming nearer, our deliverance! We are constructing a wall of sod up against one side of the shanty as a sort of air-raid shelter. We are going to pile the mattresses up on one bed and go under it when the time comes.

August 28, 1944

It was announced last night that Hospicio San Jose and Remedios Hospital will be closed, which means an addition of two hundred to our family. It was also announced that the Japs will take over the third floor of the Education Building. Much speculation is rife as to why they want the entire floor and many are of the opinion that they mean to bring in the Embassy Staff. That space has a beautiful kitchen which we have never been allowed to use. The Nips pay us a great compliment by assuming that these four walls comprise the safest spot in Manila!

This is the sort of thing that people do now: When we have *camotes* (which is seldom and then only to thicken soup) the peelings are in great demand. The vegetable workers don't peel them very finely and people fry them! Say they are delicious. Then there was our "burned rice" line now, alas, a thing of the past. When the rice is cooked in those huge covers, it always burns at the bottom. This thick, hard crust of rice used to be given out and really, Mother, to see some of

Manila's leading citizens standing in line for a piece of burned rice was a lesson in social democracy! When the rice was toasted it was very crisp and palatable. They had to stop giving it out as our ration of rice is so small now that they found they could put the burned rice into our bread and thus save on raw rice.

September 9, 1944

It is 5:15 p.m. The downtown "alert" siren has just gone off. Is it the real thing this time or not? This afternoon at three o'clock we had an air raid drill so it was a little surprising to hear the siren just now. We're keeping very calm and waiting with baited breath.

September 14, 1944

Nothing happened! But it was a real alert all right and lasted until Monday morning when it was called off. On Tuesday it sounded again and we still are "on the alert". This morning at eight o'clock the sirens wailed—a real air-raid this time. We heard no bombs and the all-clear sounded at 9:00. At 10:00 the sirens went again and lasted another hour. So we feel that this time the end is really approaching. Something is happening somewhere and although we have yet to hear the bombing with our own ears, we know we don't have long to wait. How exciting all this is! Richard asked where the American soldiers were! Poor lamb, he expected them right away!

September 18, 1944

Still waiting! I hope our deliverance will come in time, for by the end of next month our position will be truly desperate. By the 5th of October, our beef and vegetable ration which is being used in our gravy at night will be at an end. Unless the Japs bring in something we will have nothing to eat but rice, and not much of that. Our rice ration has been cut by another 150 grams and our allotment for September has not yet arrived. Furthermore, the Japs say they don't know when it will come in due to the difficulty of transportation. The doctors are so concerned over the poor state of health in camp that they voted to release stocks of corned beef individually, three ounces per person twice a week. We four, thus, get two cans a week. The cans are punched so that people must eat it and not sell or trade. This will last until the end of October.

The Japs have always resented our having reserve stocks of canned goods and in answer to our plea for more food have said; "Use up your cans. When they are finished we will provide more." Time will show! But I hope MacArthur gets here first.

September 21, 1944

Manila today received its first baptism of fire. What we have waited nearly three years for has at last come to pass—air raids! For several days we have been practicing anti-aircraft firing so that we have gotten quite used to it. This morning, shortly before ten o'clock, the practicing was going on as usual. Danny remarked that it sounded quite like the real thing and then said, "Look at those planes!" The silver glint of metal shone on our faces as we looked to the sky and saw American bomber planes flying overhead. It slowly dawned on me that it was the real thing. I got a bit panicky because Richard was in school but a few seconds later he came streaking in! We all crawled under my bed and the bombing went on. It seemed like a very heavy raid and lasted an hour.

Again at three o'clock we heard the drone and back they came for nearly two hours. We don't know, of course, but we think the damage must have been heavy. Lots of fires and lots of explosions. Tonight there was one terrific blast and the whole sky flared up. Lots of bits of shrapnel fell in the camp as well as spent shells and bullets. Two buildings had windows broken.

Well, we are all exhausted tonight but happy as we all feel that the hour of our deliverance is at hand. But I hope we have a peaceful night. The Japs shut the water off during the day which was annoying! It all seems so unreal!

September 22, 1944

More raids again this morning, starting at seven-thirty and going on till ten. There seemed to be very little resistance although there is an anti-aircraft gun uncomfortably near the camp. A shell hit the ground quite near us and a shower of dirt hit the shanty. We could even smell the cordite. So far there have been no casualties in camp although the amount of shrapnel and shells that have fallen here is considerable. All day the sky has been heavy with smoke and this afternoon there have been terrific explosions from the direction of the bay. A couple of planes few low over the camp and dipped our wings! Today's paper is supposed to have said that 2,000 planes raided Luzon yesterday. We feel almost sure that they have landed and that it may now be a matter of days! Think of it! Days! I hope we're right. The camp remains calm and we are falling into a semblance of routine.

September 23, 1944

Much water has flown under our bridges since this time last year! We thought we were excited over your leaving last September but how much more excited we are now!

No raids today although the sirens sounded this morning and we think observation planes flew over. All afternoon the Japs have been bringing in bananas, camotes, rice and corn. We were all so excited over the prospect of having corn meal in the morning instead of the eternal rice. At least we won't starve to death just yet. We have had to stop the noonday meal as the gas is out and fuel for the outside stoves is a problem. We get more mush in the morning and more rice at night to make up for it.

The children are really behaving awfully well. It is hard for them being cooped up as we are afraid to let them out of sight between raids. They don't mind the raids either. They both say they are glad as it means the war is nearly over and then we can go on a boat to see Grandma and Grandpa! This morning Alan said he was going to take his rabbit to the hospital as it had been hit by a piece of shrapnel! To think that a child of three has such words in his vocabulary.

The camp is wild with rumors, of course! Well, time will show. Our "wake-up" tune yesterday morning was "Pennies from Heaven" and this morning was "It's a Happy Day!"

September 24, 1944

Again no raids, although the sirens blew at 8:30 and the all-clear did not sound until 1:30. That is proof enough that our boys are busy somewhere near. Our days are very disorganized as we are not allowed to move about at all during alert periods. We all get on each other's nerves badly being in such a small space, but it is still better than being in the buildings. At least in the shanty we can wash and cook, but the time drags. Rumor has it that the Philippine Islands has declared war on the U. S. and that the Japs are moving out. If we only knew what was really happening and what is in store for us, but perhaps it is just as well we don't!

September 27, 1944

The last three days have been quiet with no raids. They keep blowing the alert siren off and on, and we in the camp are kept strictly to alert conditions. No music at night and no one is allowed out of the buildings or shanties after seven o'clock. It must be curfew in the Main Building. We no longer, alas, think of getting out in terms of days but have settled down to thinking "before Christmas".

October 2, 1944

Still waiting!! Camp morale is very low at the moment. The bombings were such tangible evidence that things were on the move! This lull in activity is hard to bear, especially since we are all hungry all the time. The children are all right, thank goodness.

The Annex Building had a practice fire drill this morning. Danny and several other men from this area went over with buckets. The entire Commandant's staff was there to watch and Alan (who, of course, trailed over) shouted "hello" in Japanese at them. I can't spell it but he pronounces it well. They all beamed at him and Ohashi [a Japanese civilian who knew the Chapmans before the war] spoke to Danny who told him we had heard from you. He is very friendly.

October 10, 1944

Have just received your letter of February 21st from Los Angles! It is so nice to see your writing again, and to know that you are well and putting on weight. How we envy you.

I haven't been writing much as we are all at very low ebb. We've all had heavy colds, the weather has been bad, and our friends from the sky have not been back to visit us. We did have an alert several days ago but nothing happened—here at any rate.

We are all so hungry! We've got to the state now where all we ask is a little more rice! The children each got a BANANA the other day and they were so excited. However, we have the good fortune to live next door to Santa Claus—Edgar Kneedler. He has been so kind to us. He gave us a gorgeous tongue the other day—did it taste good. He also has given us kerosene for our lamp, some white sugar, and this morning a pound of coffee. Do you know that calmansi are now 132 pesos each, and that to get one in the line is now a rare treat? We can't buy anything anymore except for things like mustard and cinnamon! They say that peanuts are 1000 pesos a kilo outside and rice is 4000 pesos a sack! Shows what inflation will do.

October 15, 1944

We have just had another air raid. The sirens went at 8:30 but nothing happened until 10:00. Sure seemed to be a lot of fighting in the air, and quite a bit of bombing. It is now 11:30 and we are waiting to see if they come back. I don't like it! I like what it stands for—deliverance—but not the bombing. I'm scared. Just now they are announcing a "recess" so that we can collect our lunch, so perhaps we can expect a respite.

October 17, 1944

No raids yesterday but the sirens blew at 8:30 this morning. It is now 10:00 and we are still waiting. The Japs pay us a great compliment inasmuch as our grounds are crowded now with their trucks and cars seeking shelter! They know darn well that this is the safest area in Manila. Incidentally, there has been a lot of excitement in camp recently. The Japs have taken over the whole of the front area from the plaza to the gates, and this space is crowded with huge packing cases and all sorts of junk. They work at it during the night and are frightfully noisy. We are forbidden to go near under pain of being shot. When the Committee protested we were told to mind our own business, they did not regard this as a civilian internment camp but as a war prisoner's camp. How I hope they pay for all of this! What a joke they make out of international law! No idea of honor and decency.

To amuse the children during this trying period I have been telling them about all the lovely food we will have afterwards. I should hate to be snuffed out without a decent meal first! Food has assumed an importance in our minds that dwarfs all others. We are so hungry! Everyone is losing weight, and nerves are strained to the breaking point. I wish I could see you now, Mother. Just the thought of seeing you and Dad again brings a lump into my throat. Well, we will meet again, and soon! They can't get us down. This is a bad bit of road but I think we'll get through safely.

October 18, 1944

It is 10:40 and we have just come through quite a raid! It only lasted about half an hour but it was noisy to say the least. I'm still shaking! We think now that these constant alerts and raids may possibly be covering up a landing but we're very cautious in our reasoning. We do know that even the paper admits a terrific bombardment of Formosa and a big naval engagement in the vicinity, but I fear that the hour of our actual deliverance has not yet struck. Well, it won't be long now. We are waiting to see if the planes come back, and trying to fix lunch in the interim. It's all very demoralizing.

(Later)

We had another very quick raid at noon, and are now still waiting (3:30). It is pouring cats and dogs and our none too roomy shanty is made still less spacious by the trunks piled up around our "shelter". Someone calls the shanty shelters "trust in God shelters" they are so primitive. Someday we shall laugh at the remembrance of our sitting here, like in a railway shelter! It isn't very funny now with two active children to keep amused. They are really very good under the circumstances.

October 19, 1944

We finished off yesterday with a quick raid at four o'clock. This morning at 7:30, without benefit of sirens, the planes seemed to drop from the clouds and we had what I consider the heaviest raid yet. A huge shell fell through a shanty, and a small shell hit a pail outside a shanty quite near us, blasting a shirt literally to pieces! The planes came over again at 10:00 and again at 1:30. It is nearly 4:00 now and I don't know whether we will have any more or not. The air raids have become a welcome, but frightful, experience. As the air raids have increased, the commandant's behavior becomes more unpredictable. He put a new rule in to effect: internees are not allowed to look up to the skies. A few in the camp have disobeyed the rule and were punished by having to stand in the hot weather, heads and necks tilted to look into the blazing sun for more than two hours.

I must say that for most of us the sunshine has been a welcome change. I managed to get a huge washing dry in between raids. Must keep clean you know! There are rumors of a landing at Atimonan but I fear the camp is one jump ahead of the news—as usual! What a queer, unreal existence this is. We do feel that the end is approaching, but I wish it would hurry. I fear this notebook won't last out! We internees are now united by one goal: to keep alive until MacArthur comes.

October 24, 1944

This has been a strange day. The alert went at 6:00 this morning, which got us all up very quickly. At 7:15 without the actual siren blowing, planes were overhead and we had a short raid. They have not come back again but we have had two more raid periods.

October 28, 1944

Nothing but wild rumors to sustain us! No more raids, not even an alert today which we have come to accept as part of our daily routine. Rumors insist that landings have been made on Luzon but we don't *know*! If only we had some concrete news to go on. The days drag and we are still hungry. Today we have received our last meat ration which has been given out individually, four ounces of Vienna Sausages. From now on we have only our own stocks of cans to draw on. That is, of course, apart from our evening meal of rice and gravy. We are lucky, inasmuch as we have enough to last us till the end of December, but many people have nothing left.

October 29, 1944

This morning, about 7:45, we saw planes overhead and were speculating as to their possible identity, when one of them went into a dive. Once again, our boys had sailed in and caught the enemy unawares. It was quite a long raid but we are now enjoying a quiet period. We heard last night of the big naval battles in the Sulu Sea and north of Luzon which have apparently delayed things here. So it was heartening to have this raid and to hope that the battle for the Philippines is on again. We have had two false starts so perhaps this time….!

I thought I would have to bring this letter to an abrupt close as I am near the end of the notebook, but I have just been given another one.

October 30, 1944

Nothing today but lots of rain! The barometer is going down, and Danny suspects a typhoon passing to the south. This will mean a further delay, I suppose. This weather is so depressing and I am so hungry tonight. It is hard to sit and wait…and wait.

October 31, 1944

As I said yesterday, the barometer was falling. By nine in the evening it was still falling and the weatherman was of the opinion that the typhoon might hit the city about midnight. A special broadcast was made warning shanty dwellers. Danny was anxious to leave the shanties because these nipa houses are not so strong. So we took the children and went to the Main Building. Fortunately we were able to get a bed but it was three-quarter size. With three of us in it we didn't sleep any too well! Danny got a bed in his old room. And nothing happened! Today is wet but no wind so I think the storm must have passed us by. Thank goodness for that. But we're STILL waiting!!

4

Hope and Hunger

We knew very little about the actions of our fighting forces during the fall of 1944. We survived during that desperate time on rumor and what little optimism we could muster.

The Allies and Japanese once considered the Philippines the backwater of the war, but it became the focus of intensive planning and attention by October 1944. The generals on both sides knew that the victor in the Philippines would control the destiny of the war. Both sides massed men, planes and materiel on the islands and waters near Leyete, at the southern end of the Philippine island chain. Over 282 warships were preparing for what was to be the largest naval battle in history.

Allied battleships opened fire on the beaches in Leyte Gulf, near the town of Tacloban, on October 20, 1944. The nearby Japanese aircraft responded immediately; they began to strafe and bomb the U.S. fleet from all sides. MacArthur and Nimitz had both been led to believe that the enemy forces in Leyte would be minimal. But the high command in Tokyo had been holding back forces, waiting for the Allies to commit to a location. Once they were certain that the Allies were headed for Leyte, the Japanese sent every available ship and plane to the area.

The Allied invasion forces overwhelmed the Japanese, despite the unanticipated level of resistance, and established a beachhead by the early afternoon of the first day of battle. MacArthur was ecstatic to be back in the Philippines and could not control his emotions long; the battle was only four hours old when he left his ship and joined the action on land. In a symbolic gesture to the Philippine population, he was accompanied by the new Philippine president, Sergio Osmena. The photograph of the triumphant MacArthur and his entourage, wading through the water, instantly became one of the most famous photographs in history.

MacArthur and Osmena were ecstatic as they touched Philippine soil. It was a personal victory for MacArthur, a fulfillment of the promise to return that he made to his adopted country three years earlier. MacArthur used his mobile radio to address the people of the Philippines for the first time since December 1941. He sent the message out over the Voice of Freedom radio and said, in part, "People of the Philippines, I have returned!" Snipers were everywhere and out of concern for his safety, MacArthur was forced to return to his carrier ship until the area was clear.

Although the Allies had established a small inroad, the battle to recapture Leyete Gulf was far from over. Leyte Gulf was a critically important location and neither side was willing to give up such precious territory easily. The U.S. Third and Seventh Fleets had a large armada poised outside the gulf, their strength evident, but they encountered a problem they could not have anticipated: a vicious and record-breaking monsoon.

The monsoon season had begun early that year and was unusually prolific. More than thirty-five inches of rain fell in the first forty days of fighting. The sailors had trouble maneuvering the air craft carriers in the soggy weather and the air corps couldn't grade the soil on Leyte to build landing strips. One of MacArthur's first objectives had been to build the landing areas so that his ground troops would have air cover as they fought to recapture the islands. Instead, the inclement weather stranded the pilots on the carriers; the majority of their flights were scrapped.

The situation did not improve once the rains slowed. The ground was so waterlogged that it remained impossible for the men to grade the air strips. The aircraft carriers continued their positions at sea longer than planned so the pilots could provide air support when the weather allowed. To compound the problems that MacArthur and Nimitz ran into, Leyte experienced three typhoons and an earthquake that same month.

Kamikaze strikes, organized Japanese suicide attacks, became another impediment for the Allies. The sailors on board the ships found the *kamikaze* strikes unbelievably frightening. It was impossible for the sailors to tell whether a Japanese Zero plane would drop bombs or whether the plane might *become* the bomb. When the *kamikazes* crashed their planes on a ship, showers of metal, bombs, gasoline and the body parts from the dead pilots rained all around the men. Over 1,000 U.S. troops were killed or injured as a result of *kamikaze* attacks during the battle for the Philippines.

The U.S. Navy continued to assault the Japanese ships despite the weather and the *kamikaze* attacks. The overwhelming size of the U.S. flotilla was no match for the Japanese. Over one third of the Japanese fleet, twenty-five ships, was sunk by the time the battle in Leyte Gulf ended on October 25. In addition, more than 65,000 Japanese troops had been killed on land and at sea. The U.S. Naval fleet lost just six ships. It was such a resounding victory that the Japanese air and naval forces were never again at a level to challenge the Allied forces. Most significantly, the critical supply lines between Tokyo and the Japanese fleet in the southern Pacific Ocean had been cut; fuel and food would be in short supply throughout the Japanese Empire from this point forward.

The Allies ended the confrontation in Leyte on December 5, beating back a final offensive launched by the Japanese. The war was over on Leyte by Christmas; there were no Japanese soldiers left on the island. Allied troops now focused on the main objective: Luzon. MacArthur planned to enter Luzon at Lingayen Gulf, the same location the Japanese had entered almost three years prior.

Lingayen Gulf is one hundred miles north of Manila and the Army had already mapped out the safest route to the capitol. MacArthur was concerned about the soldiers and citizens held captive on Luzon. He told his troops to do whatever was necessary to get to the people of Manila and especially to those of us in the camps. There was sound reasoning for his concern. In Leyte, MacArthur had been contacted by the local guerilla forces and told of a new "policy" the Japanese had adopted regarding prisoners of war. In August, the War Ministry in Tokyo had issued orders to all commandants of war camps that they were to dispose of all prisoners, leaving no trace behind, as soon as the war intensified in their geography. Although the intent of their directive was military POW camps, the history of how the Japanese had treated civilians in other territories led MacArthur to believe that the internees of Santo Tomas, Los Banos and other civilian camps were equally in peril.

We got word in camp of the Leyte landing through the secret radio. We were overjoyed and began to make plans in earnest for what we would do upon our release. Some of our neighbors were so confident that our rescue was just weeks away that they devoured the Red Cross food reserves they had been hoarding.

The news of advancing Allied troops stirred Hayashi to new levels of retaliation. The guards began to slap us in the face for any infraction. They intensified their inspections of our living quarters. Several prisoners had been taken from the camp after these inspections and had not returned. A guard burst through the entry of our shanty one morning as I was writing in my diary. I slowly got up from my chair and placed my notebook on the table beside me, terrified that he would notice it. I watched as he searched our food stock and under our beds, contemplating what my fate might be if he found the diary entries. Suddenly, the guard turned and walked out as abruptly as he had entered. I fell into my chair, my nerves completely shattered.

We thought that our food situation could not get any worse but Hayashi found ways to further deprive us. He cut our daily rations so that by November most of us were subsisting on a diet comprised primarily of rice and corn. To make matters worse, Hayashi ordered the guards to turn away food at the fence that was sent to us by sympathizers on the outside.

The camp school was closed in November because the students and teachers were so lethargic and hungry that they didn't have the energy to attend. The insufficient diet took its toll on the general health of the camp population. Previously the elderly and infirm had succumbed to disease but now more and more cases of tuberculosis, beriberi (a vitamin B deficiency), dengue fever and dysentery were being diagnosed. The death rate soared.

Prior to October 1944 the camp had averaged seven deaths per month. The fatalities in camp numbered fifteen in November and seventeen in December. And it only got worse. Our poor diets made many people in camp susceptible to the dreaded diseases and we did not have the stamina or strength to fight them off. The saying around the camp was, "if MacArthur doesn't get here soon, he'll be here in time to bury the last internee."

November 3, 1944

Dear Mother:

The food is getting sparser and less appetizing as the camp stocks of canned goods dwindle. There have been a lot of deaths among the old timers, and lots of sickness in all age groups. This is what Danny calls the "period of belt tightening".

We are largely dependent on our own resources for vegetables. The lowly *talinum* is much in demand as well as *camote* greens. The latter we regard as a delicacy and you should hear Richard cry for more! We fry them with garlic—oh yes, we are all confirmed garlic eaters now as we can get no onion! They help to stretch a meager helping of rice. It's not easy, this constant hunger.

We are no longer able to get any sort of margarine. I am so desperate for cooking fat that I sometimes cook our *talinum* in my cold cream. Imagine!

November 5, 1944

Planes came over this morning at 7:45 and we had a brisk raid. They came over again later for a brief time. It is now ten and we expect them over any time. I hope this means they are ready to start landing on Luzon.

November 6, 1944

Very tired tonight. The siren blew at 4:30 this morning, which is slightly early for me! We thought we heard bombing far away in the distance but there was nothing here. Just after breakfast, however, they came over with one of the heaviest raids we have experienced so far. Another raid at 12:30; it was short and mild.

The raids themselves are rather nasty as so much shrapnel and shells fall in this area. The camp is surrounded with anti-aircraft guns and the sound of their firing is much more terrifying than the bombs which we know are falling at a safe distance. A shell exploded in a shanty right next to Tommy's and several pieces of shrapnel fell in his shack but no serious damage was done. The "between" periods are hard on the nerves.

Sentries are posted all over the grounds and no movement is allowed unless absolutely necessary. If one has to go to the bathroom one must shout "Benjo" [toilet] to the sentry and he allows you to pass. This is only when the raid is temporarily over, of course. They are frightfully strict about anyone standing in the open during raids, and several men who were trying to watch the raids have been taken to the gate and kept standing in the sun all day as punishment. The sentries have been told they are responsible for our safety, you see, and they don't like having anyone move about.

Somehow we get through the days, buoyed up by the hope that we are nearing the end. I got a lot of sewing done today. You would be surprised at what I have learned to do. Necessity you know! I made myself a nightgown and it has turned out quite well. I have also made a pair of shorts out of an old pair of Danny's trousers, and another pair and blouse from my old red housecoat. I had a kind friend cut them out but I did all the sewing.

The Japs seem bent on making life harder just now with all sorts of petty restrictions. For instance, we used to be able to sit down during roll call but now we are forbidden to take our chairs out and must all stand at attention—children as well—for the twenty or twenty-five minutes both morning and evening. Then there is the question of bowing. They have been trying to make us bow for a long time but now they are really enforcing it. At roll call we must practice bowing from the waist so that when the Japs inspect us we can really perform gracefully. The commandant has given us as a reason for the standing and bowing that roll call is a ceremony and must be treated as such.

Tonight they have made a broadcast about this all-important question of bowing. The commandant stated that as we are being held in *safe-keeping* according to the international agreement, we must show our gratitude to the chivalry of the Japanese Army by bowing on all occasions to the officers and soldiers.

International agreement! How glibly they quote it when we are being nourished on a diet which any self-respecting farmer would hesitate to give to hogs! I'd better not get started.

This afternoon, as a special treat, we opened a small can of concentrated orange juice from the comfort kit and gave the children a little. They did enjoy it! But, Master Alan, when my back was turned, drank almost half the can! I was so angry and so afraid he would be sick but he has gone to bed without any ill effects. Poor lambs, they are so hungry that they will eat anything.

November 7, 1944

Election Day! I hope Roosevelt gets in again. No excitement so far today although the alert is on. Let's hope we are pounding them somewhere.

November 9, 1944

Horrible today. Lots of wind and rain, as there is a typhoon knocking about. The barometer is very low and shows no tendency to rise. The weather experts think it may miss us but it is approaching Luzon and this will, of course, keep up until it passes. I do think we have enough to bear just now without having the weather conspire against us! November is such a horrible month with all these typhoons. Oh, if we get out of this safely, I hope we will never see the tropics again. I've had enough of the "glorious East."

November 10, 1944

Well, we had quite a nasty time of it yesterday. The barometer (Danny's most precious possession) kept on dropping until it reached the "Severe Hurricane" section. Toward evening it steadied and even rose a little as the typhoon passed to the north, so we thought the worst was over. However, the wind began to rise and increased in intensity about 10:00. It was very nerve-wracking so we bundled up the children and our mattresses and went to the building. We were able to sleep in the ironing room. Lots of people came in and joined us. That's the only drawback to shanty life. The wind howled all night but the majority of the shacks seemed to stand the strain. Today is still blowy but dry so we are back to normal again. Let's hope this is our last experience of this kind. I do like my own bed!

November 13, 1944

Bombing started at 7:30 a.m., with the siren rather belatedly sounding afterwards, and it has kept up pretty steadily all day. The longest quiet period was at noon so that we were able to have lunch in peace. This afternoon was the heaviest yet (that is, the nearest to us) when all hell seemed to let loose about us. The shanty shook with the vibration and the shrapnel fell about the camp like hail. Dear Lord, let our deliverance come soon! This business of spending one's entire day crawling in and out of shelters and wondering if "that one has your name on it" is nerve-wracking to say the least!

There are big fires in the direction of the bay which seems to have gotten a pretty thorough working over. Now it is 4:30 and we are all tired, dirty and *very* hungry. Dinner is not being served until 6:00 so we have quite a wait still. It is really a lesson in psychology to see how we fall upon the most repulsive messes and eat them with the utmost avidity, looking hungrily about for any crumbs which may have escaped our eager fork! All is grist that comes to our mill these days. Tell Jack that the days of *talinum* and duck eggs seem like a rosy dream to us who have not tasted eggs for many a month. Even the despised *talinum* is served in scanty portions. All our conversations are on the subject of food and during raids the children beg me to recount stories of food "when the war is over."

I am always reminded nowadays of Scarlet O'Hara (have you read "Gone with the Wind" yet, Mother?) and that bit where she vows that "I'll never go hungry again, not if I have to lie and cheat and steal for it." Also there's a bit of song she quotes about "Just a few miles to tote the weary load." Our "few miles" are becoming harder and harder to bear. Perhaps I sound a bit light-headed but this has been quite a day. It is amazing how the children display no signs of fear whatever. They get restive, of course, and start quarreling, but they display touching confidence in their parents during the actual raid.

November 14, 1944

We've been bombed practically all day. The sirens got in their word first at 7:30 and the first raid began at 8:00. It is nearly 4:00 now and this is the first time the sky has been clear. It's exhausting and nerve-wracking but it is bringing us closer to the end—we hope.

Such a pleasant surprise just now when our supervisor brought me your letter of May 25th. So glad to hear you are in touch with Danny's mother. We are at a loss to know who "Marie" is with her second daughter but we think you must mean Danny's sister, Maenie. If it is her I am delighted to hear the news and very complimented at having a namesake. It seems so funny to hear from you at this stage of the game. Oh, I do hope we will be together soon.

November 18, 1944

No raid since the 14th and the camp is correspondingly gloomy. The Japs have been feeling the strain too. Up to now we have been able to supplement the Army ration of cereal from our own reserves. Now we are at an end so we will have a further reduction in our already slender ration. The Commandant blandly admits that the military ration is insufficient but says there is nothing that can be done about it. Added to all this is the lack of tobacco which people are feeling the effect of terribly. A smoke is a good thing when you are hungry. We've been lucky inasmuch as Danny traded a watch for several packages of tobacco. He rolls our cigarettes using newspaper or anything we can find but that will soon be at an end. I can't think of any punishment severe enough for the lousy, dirty.........!!!!!

The old people are dying like flies. We have an average of two deaths a day now. To balance the deaths we have a birth rate increase coming along nicely. I feel so sorry for anyone having a child under these circumstances. I heard about one young, unmarried girl who is having a baby next month. I understand her parents have rather cast her off and that she has nothing for the offspring. I made a package of diapers, camises and one or two jackets and sent it to her. She has just been round to thank me, poor child. She was so grateful.

November 20, 1944

Yesterday's thirteen-hour air raid broke all records. It wasn't nearly as bad as it sounds, however. The day started with the siren's wail at 6:00 and we heard distant bombing. Nothing happened very near the city, although there were spasmodic raids all day, mostly in the direction of the bay and Cavite. It was very tiring, though, sitting and waiting for something to happen. The all-clear didn't go until after 7:00 p.m. and we were so tired that we went to bed early.

Today has been quiet, for which I am rather glad as Danny has unexpectedly come down with bacillary dysentery. What a time for this to happen. I've been running around all morning to clinics and labs, getting him started on the cure. Fortunately, he doesn't feel very sick. It's hard to keep him on the right diet under the circumstances. Tonight we will have bouillon and soup powder so I can keep him going on that.

Incidentally, the rumor of more comfort kits is rapidly gaining ground in the camp. The paper actually stated that they have arrived in Kobe [Japan] and would be distributed as soon as possible. But, there is a lot of water between here and Japan. God knows we need them. It would be wonderful to have some supplies in. The Japanese have suggested that we round up the dogs and cats in the camp and eat them. Can you imagine anything more horrible?! I understand that some people have actually done so already but I don't feel hungry enough yet.

November 21, 1944

The damn siren went at 4:30 this morning. It is now 10:00 and we are still waiting. Danny was up most of the night and feels very weak and wretched. I am keeping him in bed and think he is now a little better. Oh, damn the Japs!

November 28, 1944

We had raids off and on during Saturday, the 25th, but nothing since. The camp has come to regard even bombing with apathy. We are all so hungry that one can think of nothing but food. There is a mad rush on now to plant anything to supplement our meager diet. Every square inch of ground is being plowed up and people are planting *talinum* and other greens that grow fast. People are eating hibiscus leaves, canna roots and banana shoots. The roots are rather stringy and tasteless but the banana shoots are not bad. You never saw such a food-conscious community!

Danny is much better but is so thin that he is a pathetic sight. His clothes hang on him! He only weighed 118 lbs. before the dysentery and what he weighs now I shudder to think. I am down to 110 but feel well and keep going. The children are remarkably well, thank God. We know this can't go on forever, but this particular period is three times as long as our whole three years of internment have been. It's awful to contemplate another Christmas in here but I guess we have to face it.

December 3, 1944

No raids, no nothing! I think the camp is at its lowest ebb. It may be that we can go lower but I doubt it. With our troops only an hour away (as the plane flies) our actual deliverance seems just as much a mirage as it did in 1942. Of course, a great deal of our depression can be laid quite naturally on the fact of our hunger. The very fact that the one absorbing topic of the day is the "comfort kit" story shows how great our devotion to the great god, Stomach, is. Everyone is discussing the pros and cons of the case. The kits are here—they are in the bay—they are on the way—the prisoners in Bilibid have ours—they have such and such in them—certain friends of the Japanese are smoking fresh American cigarettes....they say, they say, they say! However, today we did hear that yesterday's paper announced the arrival of relief supplies in Manila. Oh, I hope it is true and that we do get them. I'm so hungry!!

Yesterday was Danny's birthday. 37 and he weighs 115 lbs! He feels weak and depressed, and not like his usual energetic self. We are out of tobacco which does not help matters! How long, oh Lord, how long? It isn't very easy, these days, but if one can just live from hour to hour it's not too bad. We read a lot and you know how books were always a panacea for most evils in our family!

Another 150 people (over fifty years old) are being transferred to Los Banos rather unexpectedly. I think I forgot to mention that in March there was a big transfer up there of men, women and children.

December 8, 1944

Happy birthday, Jack! I'll not forget your twentieth birthday three years ago. I'm sure you're enjoying yourself today and wish I could be on hand to have a slice of that cake which I'm sure Mother is making for you.

Well, we are still waiting. No comfort kits yet and no news. The story still persists and people are firmly convinced that we will get them. They would be a blessing straight from Heaven.

I have had dengue fever and have felt rotten. I suffered from fever, chills, back ache and painful joints. I am now down to 105 lbs. I don't mind losing weight but hate this weakness that is attacking us all. Our diet is now: Breakfast, one scoop of mush (no more coconut milk, no coffee or tea except occasionally, no bread). Lunch, one scoop of lugao (rice, soft-cooked in lots of water). Dinner, one scoop of rice or corn, and a little gravy. The Japs have suddenly started bringing in soy beans from which our gravy is made. It is a great help and we hope it keeps up. Some of us can supplement this with cans or whatever we can grow. We four make one can of corned beef last three days! But think of the people, and there are many, who have nothing. No wonder the older group is collapsing or quietly dying! If the kits are actually here, the Japs are guilty of one more wanton crime by holding them up because every day makes a difference.

We now have total blackouts as there was a slight raid the other night. Curfew is at 7 p.m. and by 8:00 all shaded lights must be out. We are all getting plenty of sleep!

December 15, 1944

We are wondering if this time it is the real thing. Hope springs eternal. The all-clear was not sounded last night, we had a strict total blackout and there was a plane overhead nearly all night. Due to the blackout, the cooking of the morning mush could not be done during the night as this is all done in the outside kitchens. So for breakfast we had a piece of hard-tack or "Emergency biscuits" which have been prepared in the camp for just such a time. They are fairly substantial but as a substitute for mush, well, I'll take bacon and eggs! Fortunately, the children had mush as theirs is prepared inside the Annex kitchen.

December 17, 1944

Raids continued throughout yesterday, making it our third consecutive day. Rumors are rife but it does seem as though a landing on Luzon is either pending or actually a fact. We are already getting accustomed to this topsy-turvy method of existence. The Japanese are very strict about our staying indoors so we are more than ever prisoners. We can't even go to the tap except during "recess" periods. Up in the morning at 6:30, a rush to get the shelter fixed, washing done, all containers filled, and then a rush to get breakfast. Then we sit and wait! It is frightfully tiring but we are all so much more hopeful. We are trying hard to do something for Christmas for the sake of the children. Richards understands that Santa Claus can't come "because of the raids" and that every day will be Christmas when we get out. He is very sensible about it—he is really improving now. He is making chains out of scraps of old Christmas paper to hang on the tree.

It is Alan who gives us more trouble now. He hates confinement and can't amuse himself with drawing or cutting out as Richard can, so he proceeds to make life difficult for us all. He never stops talking. Words like "shrapnel", "camouflage", "anti-aircraft", etc. trip lightly off his tongue. He can now show you exactly the direction of the various air fields. Out of a clear blue sky he remarked, during a raid, "When are we going to start winning this war?" Not bad for a three year old! He is always hungry, or says he is, and still sucks his thumb.

The comfort kits would make a big difference to us just now so I hope the Japs will bring them in—but I very much doubt it. They read out messages from the Canadian and International Red Cross the other evening, but where are our kits? The camp is very low on rice and firewood but, of course, our men can't go out to get any rice right now. We cook on wood as there is no gas, and we have to fetch our own wood. Men go out with the push carts (under guard), walk about three miles, and then push the carts laden with firewood back to camp. It is a heavy detail. Even coconuts are no more and if we don't get the rice in we will be out of luck. MacArthur had better hurry!

December 20, 1944

We have had no more raids since I last wrote. The city is apparently still under air raid conditions as the all-clear has not sounded. We in the camp have been allowed to move around. Hope is still high, though, as we know they have landed in Mindoro and we feel that our time is coming, and soon.

This will indeed be a different Christmas to last year or the year before. No music, no entertainment, no excitement—and no food! The Japs have graciously given permission for a little candy to be purchased for the children so all the parents have contributed to a fund for same. I don't expect they will get much but even the sight of a piece of candy will send them into hysterics of delight. The presents we have contrived out of literally nothing are rather pathetic, but luckily children are not critical and we can get a certain amount of Christmas spirit anyway. For Richard, Danny has made a wooden airplane and a coloring book. He has spent a lot of time over the latter, drawing all sorts of pictures and I think R. will like it. I made him a tablecloth for his table—he is fussy about such things so I thought a cloth all of his own would please him. Then I have contrived Indian head-dresses for both boys. I also have made for Alan a bib and runner set and a

Raggedy Andy doll. A friend cut it out for me and I made it, stuffing and all. I'm rather proud of it, to tell you the truth. Then we made him a scrapbook out of some old magazines which were a gift. Poor kids, I hope we can make it up to them some day.

You would laugh to see the amount of sewing I do nowadays. Patching sheets and clothes is an old story to me. I borrowed a machine and mended Danny's blanket, with his assistance! Well, well, all valuable experience I'm sure!

Christmas Eve, 1944

My dear, very dear, Mother and Father:

It is pouring with rain, the shanty is leaking, we are all hungry—but it is Christmas Eve, 1944! Danny and the boys are decorating the "tree" and the shanty; it is all very festive. It is a queer sort of Christmas but our last, our very last, in captivity!

Our gift from the Japanese was another cut in our cereal ration to 200 grams per day per head. This, with our gravy, gives us 800 calories a day. There is nothing for the hunger but firm endurance and believe me, we have needed to dig down to new levels of endurance. Our morning mush is served after roll call and our evening meal at 4:00. We save part of the mush and eat it at noon with a few shreds of corned beef and whatever greens we can gather from our little garden.

Poor little Alan can't understand why he can't have more to eat and cries constantly from hunger. Richard, on the other hand, seems to have turned over a new leaf and is unbelievably good and patient. He never complains but takes whatever he is given. But he is so thin and his face has a pinched look that upsets me. I hope we can make it all up to him soon, poor wee lamb. Danny is a walking skeleton but keeps cheerful. I don't know what our weight is as the Japs have removed our scale, but my clothes are hanging on me.

Yesterday the most beautiful sight we have yet witnessed in the sky occurred when a huge group of American land-based planes flew over, shining like silver. They only dropped a few bombs so we conclude that they were on their way to a bigger objective. There was heavy bombing last night and the siren blew this morning, though nothing happened here.

The Japs seem to be in a villainous frame of mind. They conducted a search of shanties and buildings yesterday and put Grinnell and Duggleby [two members of the Executive Committee] in jail. No one knows why. Efforts have been made to send us in food from the outside but they have been turned aside. They did allow some mongo beans and cigarettes to come in. It is criminal to think that they have turned away <u>food</u>! I feel so bitter that I do not dare trust myself on paper.

Christmas Day, 1944

Merry Christmas! Contrary to all expectations, Danny and I have agreed that it is the happiest Christmas we have ever experienced because our sense of appreciation has been so sharpened that every simple thing has appeared in a roseate hue. This Christmas season, watered by the tears of desperation and despair and enriched with a feeling of great hope for a brave new future in a brave new world, is a Christmas which we shall always remember.

The day started right for us with the "wake-up" tune which, instead of being a Christmas carol, was "Onward Christian Soldiers". This fine old hymn with its real significance made us both feel very teary! The children were so pleased with our simple gifts that it was a delight to watch them. I managed to get to the Communion service at which Father Mattocks officiated, and his simple prayer for peace in the hearts of all men and thanks for our deliverance thus far was very stirring.

Everyone at roll call was happy and smiling for our best Christmas gift was from Uncle Sam. Last night leaflets were dropped, many of which fell into camp. This is the message they bore: "The Commander-in-Chief, officers and men of the American forces of liberation in the Pacific extend to our Loyal Allies, the People of the Philippines, the blessings of Christmas and the realization of our fervent hopes for the New Year." Isn't that a lovely message? We were so thrilled!

Breakfast consisted of coffee, mush and sweetened chocolate coconut milk—nectar beyond compare! Directly afterwards the children went to the Playhouse, where Dave Harvey had arranged a special program for them. They all got a piece of bukayo (coconut) candy which thrilled them as only sugarless kids could be thrilled.

We had callers all morning. Our lunch today was vegetable soup made from our own garden stocks together with soy bean gravy from the line, lugao, and corned beef and pudding. The last I made with mush, rice, flour, coconut milk and cinnamon. Our gift from the camp was a spoonful of jam and 15 grams of chocolate. We put jam on the pudding and poured chocolate milk over it and we all agreed it was the most *divine* dessert we had ever had! Tonight we are having fried rice (extra portions) and the kids get cake and milk.

December 31, 1944

Things have been quiet since Christmas. There has been, I'm glad to say, a slight improvement in the food inasmuch as we have been getting a small portion of soy bean soup at lunch time. This is a big help. Also, a lot of *camotes* have come in and these are such a welcome addition to our diet. Last night we had mashed camotes and gravy for supper, such good portions that we really felt full! Danny and I keep our 4:00 meal now, warm it up and have it by lamplight about 6:30. It is so much nicer and seems more civilized. Our Christmas dinner of fried rice was delicious, incidentally, and was plentiful. We topped it off with the remainder of our pudding and, with the cigarettes which we received, rounded out a pleasant day.

Poor Danny had a recurrence of his dysentery and has been so miserable. He is better now, thank goodness, and can come off the diet of lugao and greens. He weighs 107 lbs. now. Poor darling, how I shall enjoy fattening him.

New Year's Eve! Well, we have great hopes for 1945. The Japs are going to celebrate, evidently, but for the last time. I hope. We are having fried rice tomorrow with fresh beef gravy—600 kilos of caribou meat came in for us. They have also given us a ration of tobacco. Aren't they kind! At any rate, we now have a month's supply in camp so we can face the "deluge," be it a siege or whatever is in store for us. We feel it coming soon, now, the landing on Luzon and hope our share won't be too exciting!

5

The Beginning of the End

The U.S. Fleet sailed out of Leyte at the end of December 1944 and headed toward the Lingayen Gulf in northern Luzon. They had easily recaptured the islands of Mindoro and Marinduque, southwest of Luzon by January 3. As they raced toward Lingayen Gulf, the Allies girded for the battle to retake Manila and liberate the people of the Philippines. MacArthur prepared to wage a decisive battle against an enemy he assumed would heavily defend its prize possession. In preparation, the Allies brought ships, planes and troops in massive numbers to the area: 164 ships, 3,000 landing craft and 280,000 men. It was all unnecessary. They entered Lingayen Gulf under sunny skies on January 9, 1945. There were no Japanese forces in sight.

Yamashita had planned the total lack of resistance to the Allied landing. He had been closely following the events of the Leyte Gulf, Mindoro and Marinduque conflicts and knew that his men and materiel were outnumbered. When he learned that U.S. forces were headed to Luzon, he left the majority of troops in Manila to defend the city and moved his command headquarters north to Baguio. Yamashita had little choice in his defense strategy, given the reduced strength of the Japanese armada and air force. His only option was to concentrate his forces in Bagio and Manila.

MacArthur quickly established a beachhead and began making plans for the re-capture of Manila. The fastest route from Lingayen Gulf to the capital city was through the central plain of Luzon. The troops would be required to maneuver through rugged, mountainous terrain for the first eighty-five miles of the trip, and marshy bogs for the final fifteen miles, before reaching the outskirts of Manila. It was a difficult task because their tanks and jeeps were not equipped for the terrain. The added dimension of enemy troops and snipers made it all the more treacherous, but MacArthur was on a mission.

Shortly after he landed on Luzon, guerilla forces told him of the merciless slaughter of Allied POWs on December 14 on the Philippine island of Palawan, some 250 miles southwest of Manila. MacArthur was convinced that the Japanese were beginning to carry out the August directive from the War Ministry to kill all prisoners of war. The guerillas also told MacArthur that five hundred American soldiers, many of whom were survivors of the Bataan Death March, were being held in a prison camp near Cabanatuan. The guerillas reported that these men had been severely tortured and were riddled with disease.

At the end of January, General Walter Krueger, one of MacArthur's top aides, decided to attempt a rescue of the Cabanatuan POWs and dispatched a company of men to launch a surprise attack. Krueger believed that time was of the essence; if the example on Palawan Island was any indication, the Japanese were becoming frantic and savage in their response to the advancing U.S. troops.

MacArthur's senior staff wanted to delay the advance into Manila until they were more certain of Japanese positions and troop strength. MacArthur was adamant that Manila and we prisoners in Santo Tomas be liberated immediately. He ordered his troops to "go around the Japs, bounce off the Japs, save your men, but get to Manila! Free the internees of Santo Tomas!" How MacArthur knew that the lives of the internees of Santo Tomas were in peril was due to an internee by the name of Ernest Stanley.

Stanley was the most hated man in Santo Tomas. He was a British internee who claimed to be an English missionary and was made the official interpreter when the camp first opened. We were all aware of his apparent fondness for the Japanese; he ate, slept and lived with them in their quarters. We referred to him sarcastically as "Stanley-san."

Unbeknownst to us, Stanley was a British Intelligence officer, sent into the camp to monitor the activities of the Japanese. Because of his close relationship with the Japanese, Stanley had unbridled access to the commandant's office. In late December he had been conversing with Hayashi in his office and saw an order from the War Ministry instructing Hayashi to place all the male internees into one building and blow it up. The women and children were to be taken out and used as hostages when the American troops marched into Manila.

Stanley got word of the plan to a Japanese-American spy who was on guard duty at the gate. He, in turn, got word of the plan to execute us to the local guerilla force who communicated the information to MacArthur. The knowledge that many of his former friends and associates in Santo Tomas were slated for a grisly death propelled MacArthur to demand the urgent race to Manila.

Paradoxically, just as the Americans were moving closer to Santo Tomas, we were about to give up hope. Although we could hear the planes overhead and bombing in the city, we were too hungry to pay much attention. Hollow-eyed and stick thin, we had been waiting for almost three months for liberation. We were beginning to think that the day would never come.

Hayashi ordered all of us into the Main building one morning after breakfast. Danny and I were certain that they were going to kill us. Strangely, we were almost apathetic about it and took some solace in the fact that the four of us would die together. After an hour of waiting, Hayashi ordered the guards to let us out. In retrospect, I wonder if it was a dress rehearsal for the executions he had been ordered to carry out.

We all suffered some symptoms of malnutrition by the beginning of 1945. Our gums were swollen, our mental acuity was lessened and we had pain in our bones. The internees that suffered the most were those that contracted dysentery or beri-beri, compounding their physical ailments. The Japanese continued to reduce our rations in the food line. Our intake on a typical day consisted of one ladle of watery mush for breakfast, one ladle of watered-down soy bean soup for lunch and a *camote*-bean-rice stew for dinner (mostly flavored water, with a few bits of food). These meals provided us with approximately eight hundred calories a day.

Illness and death were becoming commonplace to us. Thirty-two people died in January, nearly twice as many as in December. People walked the campus with a middle-distance stare, shuffling from place to place. Danny and I stopped most of our socializing because keeping up our end of a conversation tended to sap our energies. Mostly, we sat in our shanty, too listless for any activity except for trips to the food line.

The Executive Committee required that we continue to weigh ourselves each month. In January, after three full years of captivity, they calculated that the men had lost an average of fifty-one pounds and the women had lost an average of thirty-two pounds. The elder population suffered the most dramatic weight loss, averaging fifty-eight pounds for the men and fifty-three pounds for women.

The camp doctors began to write "starvation" or "malnutrition" as the cause of death on the death certificates. Hayashi ordered them to refrain from the practice, but the doctors refused and resigned their posts rather than compromise their feelings about the conditions in camp. The Executive Committee pleaded with Hayashi for additional food but he told them we were on the same rations as the Japanese guards. It was a preposterous statement given the rotund stature of the guards, but Hayashi never relented and we continued to subsist on inadequate fare.

There was no escaping the fact that the Japanese were intending to kill us, either by savagery or starvation. We were facing certain death unless the Army could reach us first.

January 6, 1945

Dear Mother and Dad:

Well, bombing started again today. For the past week or so, there have been American planes overhead every day, and we have heard bombing in the distance. But today they have really gone to town on the local airports. Hope is running high for we all feel that the landing on Luzon could take place at any time. It can't come any too soon.

Although the food is a little better, we are hungry all the time and it's not pleasant. Richard weighs 52 lbs. He weighed 56 lbs. on his birthday last August so you can see why I am worried about him. He is in the first stages of malnutrition, according to the doctor and shows it by listlessness. Alan keeps up pretty well. I weigh 103 and am experiencing difficulty in keeping skirts or shorts on! However, we are optimistic and feel sure the end is approaching.

Yesterday Messrs. Grinnell and Duggleby were removed from the camp jail and taken out—where or why, no one knows.

We are allowed to draw our entire daily ration from the camp raw if we so desire, and we have been doing this. We have to make our own mush (no more corn, worse luck) and we like it. We can cook it ourselves so that it tastes better and goes further. *Camotes* are still coming in and they do taste so good. We all feel better fed when we have them—and do the children love them! Soon, soon, I hope we shall be eating good food again. Army beans? I hope so.

January 7, 1945

Bombing has continued throughout the day. Judging from the "noise" Grace Park in particular has been flattened.

The camp is seething with excitement. It is very evident, even to the most pessimistic observer that the Japs are preparing to leave the camp. No sentries have been posted, as is usual during air raids, to prevent movement about the camp. The soldiers have been leaving in trucks, they have been burning papers in the office and conferences are going on. Our own guards are posted around the camp and there is a general feeling in the air! The Japs have killed all their pigs and the caribou, which they have been using as a beast of burden. The condemned man's last meal! Rumors are rife, of course. We have our army at Cavite! However, something is happening. It is also said that the Japs have taken out most of our rice, leaving a four-day supply which they say is ample. I wonder, oh, I wonder.

January 9, 1945

Our fourth consecutive day of bombing. There has just been an announcement from the Commandant to the effect that to avoid bloodshed, he and his staff had planned to leave the camp, but as the situation has not yet arisen, they are still with us; that he is very concerned over our welfare particularly as regards food as there is no food in Manila. This last part is funny as while he was talking, his soldiers were busily engaged in taking rice out of our bodega. They have been doing this for the last three days, using handcarts, a car and a truck.

January 10, 1945

Our fifth day! There were several bombs dropped last night, and several raids today. This being cooped up isn't much fun but it is infinitely better than being stuck in the buildings! We think the Japs must be demolishing a lot as there are heavy explosions going on intermittently. Rumor has it that they are blowing up the bridges and the piers. It's all very exciting but I wish it were over. I long to be able to send you a cable!

We dream of food constantly. Danny and I pour over my cookbooks, plan menus and discuss food by the hour. We all feel that our appetites will never be appeased, no matter how much we eat. I'm afraid that people will be horrified at our greed when we emerge into polite society. However, when you consider that for the past four months our diet has consisted of corn, rice, *camotes*, greens and a "suspicion" of meat—no wonder! Just think, we have had no milk, eggs, meat, fruit, bread or butter; the simple essentials of a normal diet. It's going to take a lot of eating to make it up!

January 11, 1945

The sixth day! Such a thrill this morning when two planes flew over the camp, so low that for the first time we saw the insignia on their wings. You should have heard the "hum" of excitement from all internees. We know that landings have been made at San Fernando, La Union, and that heavy fighting is going on at Gamorits. There is a rumor that a large convoy is 35 miles off Corregidor. From which direction will our deliverance come, I wonder? It had better come soon. Honestly, Mother, I am so hungry tonight that with the slightest encouragement I would start howling! It's horrible to be hungry all the time. To see the kids lick their plates, literally! Hope is about the only thing that is keeping us going at the moment. My weight is down to 101 lbs. now. I'm so sylph-like.

January 12, 1945

The seventh day! No bombing in the city today but there was some at a distance. Demolition work continues. I don't know what will be left of Manila. Last night the whole sky towards the bay was illuminated by a sudden blaze which looked as though gasoline was ablaze. There have been lots of fires today, too. Strong rumors have it that there is heavy fighting going on at Naic, Cavite and all sorts of stories as to how far the troops up north have progressed. I think we can measure it by weeks now and not many of them. Most people have it down to days but we are afraid to hope so. Anything can happen now, is the feeling in which we can all share.

January 13, 1945

The eighth day! Still under air raid conditions, with curfew at 5:30, total blackout and no movement about the camp except when permission is granted at meal times.

Tommy came over this morning with a story that he had heard you have received $2.90 for every day that you were interned. I hope that is true as it must have been a help to you. And what it means to us to look forward to that! About $12,000 for us four!

January 14, 1945

The ninth day! It's a rocky road to Dublin, as we say! Something has happened to the water supply so that there is no water except at ground level. We keep everything filled wondering if it will peter out altogether. Oh, MacArthur, do hurry up! The chow tonight is the last word—just rice and watery spinach.

January 16, 1945

The eleventh day! Very heavy bombing all day in the direction of Marikina. We now have the general in charge of all prison camps in residence in Santo Tomas. He came in complete with baggage and furniture. Whether it is due to his influence or whether it is because they are preparing for a last stand, I don't know, but the Nips have been bringing in supplies of rice, corn and *camotes* all day. The fuel situation is so acute that we are now tearing up the benches and part of the dining sheds for firewood. Oh, MacArthur, do hurry up!

January 17, 1945

The twelfth day! Still under air raid conditions but today has been quiet. We hear that the Yanks are as far as Stotsenberg, but it is difficult to believe.

Poor Tommy has had an unfortunate experience. He took some Agnesia, thinking it was Magnesia! They had to use a stomach pump on him but he is quite all right today. He is really looking very well and fit, still. He is working in the Annex kitchen so fares pretty well.

A great delicacy now is *camote* peelings. These are given out to workers and people clean and scrape them. They help to fill you up, but....! Tommy has been very kind about saving some for us. I am so worried about Danny and Richard. Both so thin! Oh, these damn Japs.

January 19, 1945

The fourteenth day! Three years ago today Danny took up residence here! It's horrid today, raining and cold and dreary. No news, so everyone is correspondingly depressed.

January 23, 1945

The eighteenth day! It has poured buckets all afternoon. I keep thinking of the rainy afternoons when you used to call me over for cocoa and muffins! Was that another world, I wonder? It seems so long ago and it seems too long to wait before we will eat decent food again. It's awful to have constant visions of good food before you. It's all we can think or talk about nowadays. What wouldn't I give for a plate of your fudge?

January 24, 1945

The nineteenth day! Rather depressed because Danny now weighs 104 lbs. and I weigh 97 lbs. We've decided not to weigh ourselves again until the boys come in. One wonders how low we can possibly get. Oh, well, it can't be much longer now.

January 25, 1945

The twentieth day! The news continues to be good but we are still waiting. We are all so weak that we can't do much in the way of work. Consequently, the time does drag rather. Danny has fortunately found himself a good occupation. He is drawing plans for a model home to be built somewhere in the States. No more

East for us! Captain Francis has talked so much about Virginia that we are dying to settle there. He and Danny want to go into business together, and we have lots of fun talking and discussing plans for this glorious future to which we look forward. [The business was going to be a wine shop in Washington, D.C. called "We Wine Washington"] As for me, I can only dream of the food we'll eat! We hope and pray that the Army will take us out of here quickly and send us to the States. Then a visit to you while we make plans. It seems like a beautiful dream after the horror and nightmare of these dreadful days.

January 27, 1945

The twenty-second day! Last night we could hear artillery fire going on all night, and today we hear that there is fighting going on at Antipolo. Hope is springing up again as we draw closer. So many people are going down so rapidly that every day makes a difference. Beriberi is rampant or, rather, just plain starvation. It's awful.

January 28, 1945

The twenty-third day! The local radio (heard over the wall) announced this morning that heavy fighting is going on in Bigaa, just eighteen miles north of us. Next stop, Marilao! It is coming closer. We see flashes in the sky at night. If it would just end!

I had to weigh and measure the children today as the figures are required by the powers that be. Richard, at seven, is 4'2" and weighs 47 lbs. Alan, nearly four, is 3'4" and weighs 31 lbs. It's pitiful.

January 30, 1945

Twenty-fifth day! Richard is not so well today, running a slight fever so I am keeping him in bed. He is so thin—I am so worried about him.

Heavy bombing in the direction of Cavite and lots of demolition work going on. There is smoke over the city constantly and the weather is so queer for this time of year. Overcast and rainy. The news continues good and we can hear artillery fire constantly. We say our forces are as far as San Fernando, Pampanga, which really isn't far. I don't see how it can be much longer now, but every day counts with many of us. George Stewart, next to us, is very sick with beriberi and is flat on his back. I wonder how we will look to outsiders—pretty grim, I fancy!

January 31, 1945

Twenty-sixth day! There has been a lot of excitement today due to the fact that the Japs have raised a row over the medical situation. There were seven deaths yesterday and Dr. Stevenson, in signing the death certificates, put down the cause of death as malnutrition. The Japs considered this as "reflecting on them". As he refused to change the wording, they have put him in jail for twenty days. Fancy!

Poor little Richard is in the hospital as he has dysentery. He cried a lot when he went in, but when I went to see him in the afternoon he was quite cheerful as he was told he could have "seconds" of supper! The food is much better there so perhaps he will pick up a little. Poor wee lamb.

February 1, 1945

Twenty-seventh day! Another month starting. Well, it can't be much longer. All night there were explosions, fires, bombing, artillery fire, and shooting. They say the guerrillas are very active and well organized. Also, that the main forces are now 30 miles from the city. Patience, patience! But it's wearing thin.

February 2, 1945

Twenty-eighth day! Lots of demolition going on and bombing. We are so used to it now that we pay no attention any more. Richard is much better and very cheerful.

February 3, 1945

Twenty-ninth day! Such a thrill this afternoon when six American planes flew over slowly and so low that we could see them quite clearly. The camp went mad, cheering and waving. The Japs didn't like it a bit! Sentries went running around with fixed bayonets chasing people in. What a lift it gave us. It's down to days now, I know. Last night there was quite a battle going on east of us. There is supposed to be heavy fighting in Cavite.

9:00 p.m.

It's over, my God, it's over!! The Yanks are here! Oh, it's so exciting that I can't write but I will tomorrow. There was a lot of shooting and excitement about dusk and it continued until a roar went up from the building—and a tank came in the front gate. American soldiers. My God, it's true! At last, at last we were free. Oh, I thank God. It was so wonderful to see the tanks and the men—great big Americans! I touched one and said "Oh, is it really over?" and he said, "It is for you all, ma'am". We rushed over to the children's hospital to reassure Richard. We found him awake and so happy and excited. Then we came back to the shack and opened a can of corned beef and milk and had a party. Alan, of course, was wide awake and excited. The Japs left in camp barricaded themselves in the Education Building and the Yanks have been shooting them out! I can't wait till morning to see what happens next. Oh, it's too exciting. I still can't believe it has happened so quickly. We've got the lamp on and we are too happy to go to bed!

February 7, 1945

This is the first time that I've been able to sit down and write. So much has and is still happening that it is difficult to settle on anything. It still seems like a dream and it's all so exciting that I don't think we'll ever calm down.

We never went to bed at all that first night—we'll never forget February 3rd. We stood around talking with the soldiers. They insisted that they were just as glad to see us as we were to see them. They plied us with cigarettes and food!

What apparently happened was this: the First Cavalry (who are famous for their work in New Guinea and the Admiralty Islands) were rushed down here on direct orders from MacArthur to save us! They were afraid that the Japs would either kill us all or use us as hostages. Their orders were to stop for nothing but come directly to Santo Tomas. For three days and three nights they were on the march, ending up with a tank battle on the streets of Manila. They took the camp and waited for reinforcements to come in as Manila itself was still in the hands of the Japs. Of all the ways to end this period, we never thought of this solution!

The Japs who were caught in camp entrenched themselves in the Education Building on the first floor. The second and third floors were full of internees. Well, they tried to blast them out, but to spare the internees, they finally agreed to let the Japs go out of camp—which they did, and we understand that they were taken care of—outside!

The Beginning of the End

The prisoners reacting to the raising of the American Flag on the Main building after the First Cavalry rescued them
Photo courtesy of Dan Balkin.

February 9, 1945

It hasn't all been beer and skittles, though. The Japs are still fighting in the city and snipers have been firing at the camp. Yesterday they managed to get the camp within range and hit the Main Building and the gym. There were many wounded and many deaths. This has saddened us all so much. You know all of the dead people...it is so dreadful, so sad.

Tommy got Dad's and Jack's letter yesterday. What a thrill! Fancy Jack in the Army and Doreen in the Navy! Well, please God, we'll be together soon. They have already taken lists of those who want to go and where. We have asked to be sent to the good old U.S.A. No more East for us!

There isn't much left of Manila. The Japs have burned practically the whole city—what swine they are!

We are enjoying good food so much. Yesterday we had potatoes and the most gorgeous stew for lunch, and corned beef hash and fruit cocktail for dinner. Milk and sugar on our mush again, and today we are to have bread! The kids just can't take it all in.

Once they get the city cleaned up we'll all feel happier. Oh, and we have news broadcasts now so that we know what is going on in the rest of the world. So many old Manila men have returned with the troops.

They say we are to be taken out by plane to Leyte and then on to hospital ships just as soon as possible. I just can't wait to get started.

MacArthur arrived yesterday and we had a fine view of him.

◆ ◆ ◆

And so the diary ends. And although we were freed, we were still a long way from landing in the "good old U.S.A." The next few weeks would bring further trials and one final threat of death.

6

The American Dream

The men from the First Cavalry who liberated us were nearly all Texans. They were tough, seasoned soldiers who had experienced some of the most hellacious fighting in the Pacific theater, but they treated us with unimaginable gentleness and courtesy.

We appreciated their kindness, but nothing exceeded our excitement when they offered us three days worth of rations. The men were so horrified by our physical condition that they insisted on adding their K-rations to our stock. I reproached one of the men for giving us his food. He shook his head and said,

"Ma'am, how could we eat when we saw you people?"

Another soldier remarked that this was the first time that the war made sense to him. He said that previous to his arrival in Santo Tomas, every battle he'd fought in the jungles and mud only gained him more jungles and mud. This time he felt the satisfaction of rescuing his own people.

Richard and Alan were fascinated with the soldiers and the soldiers were very kind and patient with them in return. Richard brought five of the soldiers to our shanty one afternoon and as they entered they carefully stood their guns against the wall, sat in a circle on the floor, and gazed soulfully at me. Goodness knows I was no object of glamour! Painfully thin, shabby clothing, no makeup—to them I was still a woman! Several of the soldiers adopted us and I later wrote to their families to tell them of their sons' exemplary behavior.

One of our rescuers, Bob Holland, was not a member of the First Cav, but a Marine attached to the Army. Bob was an engineer by education who volunteered for the Marines and rose to the rank of Master Technical Sergeant. On February 3, 1945 he was stationed just outside the camp, directing the planes that bombed the area around Santo Tomas so that the tanks could make their way into the camp. Late that day, once our liberation was secured, Bob entered the camp. He was totally shocked by what he saw. Like many of his comrades, he knew nothing of Americans being held as POWs in the Philippines. His observations about our condition are telling:

> "I wandered around the Santo Tomas campus by myself and got lots of hugs from many internees, especially when they saw that I was a Marine. They hadn't seen many Marines. In strolling around the campus I met several of the internees. Like the other GIs, I was appalled at their physical condition. The men were pale and undernourished; the women looked a little better; the children, for the most part, appeared to be in good condition. It was obvious that whatever food was available went to the children."[1]

Kathleen with Bob Holland in November 2003.
Bob was responsible for directing the planes that provided air cover for the Army tanks that broke through the gates of Santo Tomas.

Hayashi and his men were taken out of the camp but the war outside the gates continued to rage for another month. The Japanese systematically destroyed what was left of Manila, bombing or burning all of the major buildings in the city. Shortly after the Americans arrived in camp, the Japanese began to shell us. We had grown used to the bombing of the previous few weeks, but the whine of the shells was more frightening still. The shelling on February 8th killed fifteen internees and wounded ninety. The deaths hit all of us in camp very hard; it

---

1. Robert Holland, *The Rescue of Santo Tomas*, (Paducah, 2003), page 82

seemed particularly devastating and unfair to have this loss of life after all that we had been through.

In mid-February, the battle in Manila was still raging and snipers were all around us. Alan was standing outside a nearby shanty with a friend of ours one afternoon when a sniper's bullet suddenly pierced our friend's knee, tearing it to shreds, just inches from Alan's head. Danny and I began to worry about getting out of the Philippines before one of us was injured or killed. We couldn't bear the thought of something happening to us before we could taste freedom.

U.S. soldiers take a break in the shanty area.
The Watson's shanty was next to the shanty on the right in this picture. The foreground is where Alan was almost killed by a sniper's bullet in February 1945.

The Allies destroyed the final Japanese garrison in Manila on February 27, but mop-up operations continued in the city for some time after the battles ended. The Army told us that it was not safe for us to leave Santo Tomas as there were Japanese holdouts and snipers hiding in all corners of the city. We had suspected as much; the noise coming from the direction of downtown Manila was constant. Danny and I were content to stay in the camp for the time being, focusing on our repatriation plans.

We abandoned our plans to move to Virginia, concluding that Danny's job prospects were better back in Scotland. We decided to sail on the ship bound for California, stay for a short time with my family in Los Angeles, and then move on to Scotland. Danny was confident that he would be able to secure a position with his former employer, Ker and Co.

Manila finally gained some semblance of normalcy in mid-March. The Americans had cleared the city of Japanese troops, so Danny and I asked one of the G.I.'s to drive us to our home in Santa Mesa. We hoped to recover as many of our possessions as possible to take with us when we left Manila. We had heard from friends that the city had taken tremendous blows during the past month but we hoped against hope that some of our belongings were still in tact.

We were quite nervous and anxious on the drive to our neighborhood but weren't prepared for what we saw as we rounded the corner onto Sociego Street: our house had been demolished. My parents' house next door was also gone. In their places were massive, jungle-like gardens. The beautifully manicured lawns and flower beds in which we had taken so much pride were overgrown tangles of burnt vines and stalks. We returned to camp, dejected by the knowledge that we had little to our names but the clothes on our backs.

The following week I decided to see downtown Manila before we left. I knew that many of the old landmarks of my childhood had been destroyed in the bombing, but I wanted one last opportunity to see the city. I took Alan with me and set out from the shanty to the Main building where we queued for rides on the military trucks. Alan ran ahead of me toward the convoy parked in front of the building and saw the car he wanted—the big command car at the front of the line. He made a beeline for the car and bounded into the back seat, much to the surprise of the officers in front. I apologized to the men, but they were thoroughly amused and offered us a ride. Alan and I rode in style all the way to downtown Manila!

Once there, I was heartbroken to see that the city had been destroyed; nearly all of the old familiar sites were gone or in ruins. To my further dismay, the neutral Swiss warehouse that contained my precious wedding gifts had been bombed into extinction. I ran into a friend who told me that the friend whose car I sold for $250 at the beginning of the war had died during the Bataan Death March. I regretted that he did not live to hear that the sale of his car had made the difference between food and starvation for us.

The first group of internees, mostly military nurses, began repatriating on February 23. We were scheduled to leave camp in early April and flown to Leyte where we would board a ship bound for the U.S. Danny and I were billeted on the "mixed marriage" ship, the "John Lykes," a ship designated to transport all of the American women internees who had married foreign husbands.

On the day that we left camp I walked the grounds of the campus for one last look at what had been our home for over three years. I was happy to be leaving such a wretched place, yet also felt a sense of pride that we had survived under such grueling circumstances. I knew then that no matter what the future held for us, Danny and I could withstand anything. When we boarded the trucks to leave the camp I turned my head away from the window and never looked back.

Alan and I left on the first convoy, with Danny and Richard two hours behind us. When I reached the dock and saw the "John Lykes" I was horrified. It was a small cargo ship, and in order to board I would need to climb up a swaying rope ladder. Still weak from malnutrition, and afraid of heights, I stood with my feet planted firmly on the dock, with Alan in my arms. A sailor finally came down to my rescue and helped us both up on deck.

Once on board, I found the situation even worse. The "Lykes" did not have the type of railings found on passenger ships; instead there were only rope lines strung across the deck. I had visions of falling overboard and worried how I was going to contain an active toddler all the way to America. The sailors escorted me to the cabin that I was to share with eight other people. There were only six bunks for the ten of us. To make matters worse, we were right next to the engine room and the noise and heat combined to make the room stifling and oppressive. Our room was so uninhabitable that my eight cabin mates decided to sleep up on deck. I elected to stay in the room; at least in the cabin I didn't have to worry about Alan falling off the deck. Danny and Richard were in the hold of the ship and slept in hammocks. Richard was seasick the first few days but finally gained his sea legs and enjoyed watching the sailors perform their duties on deck.

Our lives were bearable on the "John Lykes" because it was our transport home. Danny and I spent our time talking excitedly about what might await us there. "Home" was more symbolic than tangible to us since we had never been to the U.S. We had heard plenty of stories about it from our fellow internees, and now my family was there, but we didn't really know what to expect. One thing we knew for sure: after the horrid existence we had lived the past three years we would be happy no matter where we landed.

The "Lykes" traveled in a convoy until we reached Hollandia, New Guinea, where we tied up for three days. We were not allowed to go ashore for security reasons, which was particularly painful to me because before we left Santo Tomas I had learned from a Red Cross worker that my brother Jack was on the island. I was desperate to meet up with him but I didn't know his rank or what unit he was in. A G.I. who was traveling on leave aboard the "Lykes" offered to go ashore and find him for me. The G.I. managed to find Jack out of 5,000 servicemen on the island! Jack ran to the ship once he knew we were there, laden with gifts for us donated by the men in his unit. They were small items, cigarettes, candy bars, and such, but the gesture was touching and meant the world to us at the time. Jack and I were overjoyed to see one another, and had a wonderful afternoon catching up on all that had transpired over the past 18 months.

Four days later the "Lykes" left Hollandia alone and unescorted. It was a frightening feeling to be alone on the vast Pacific in a time of war. We saw no other ships until we berthed in Honolulu. Again, we were not allowed to go ashore; instead, we had to stay on board while Danny was questioned by the F.B.I. The U.S. government was looking for anyone who had given aid and comfort to the Japanese. Before the ship could gain entry to the United States, the "foreign husbands" on board all had to be checked out.

We passengers were all overjoyed when we left Honolulu, bound for Los Angeles. At last we were on the final leg of our journey. Three days later, the ship's alarm siren sounded at two o'clock in the morning. I rolled over, thinking it was a drill, when two sailors appeared in the doorway and assured me that it was not. I grabbed Alan and rushed up on deck where I quickly located Danny and Richard. As we looked out to sea we were shocked when we saw what all the commotion was about. A Japanese submarine was stationed just off the right side of our ship, barely visible to us.

Danny and I looked at each other in disbelief. We were certain that the sub would attack us and we knew that there was little hope for survival in the open sea. It seemed ironic that after all that we had been through, when we were within days of reaching America, that we could be snuffed out in this manner. We waited what seemed an eternity for something to happen. Slowly, very slowly, the submarine continued to pull away from our ship. Later, we were told that the reason they did not attack us was that we were a light ship going home and the Japanese would rather have attacked one outbound. Our good luck appeared to be holding.

One more bit of excitement awaited Danny and I. Richard was playing tag with some of the sailors on deck one morning when a hatch door slammed shut, catching his hand. He was rushed to the clinic, where the young doctor debated for well over an hour whether he would need to amputate a finger. Luckily the doctor determined it could be saved. Danny and I were astounded at the trials we were enduring, and prayed that we would reach the U.S. before any further mishaps occurred.

Finally, in mid-May, the "Lykes" crept up the Pacific coastline. It was a typical spring day in Southern California, where the coastline comes in and out of focus between the wisps of fog. When the captain announced, "On the port side, you will see California," everyone raced to the decks. We elbowed our fellow shipmates as we worked our way to the railing in an effort to get a better view. We peered into the mist, as the ship steamed into the busy San Pedro harbor, just south of Los Angeles, and anchored. It was a momentous occasion.

Danny and I held the children as we docked and stood silently, tears streaming down our cheeks.

At last, I was an American.

Epilogue

The mailman slid Kathleen's mail through its slot in the front door, sending it crashing to the floor and startling Kathleen from her daydream. She glanced at the clock on her desk and was surprised that over an hour had passed. She looked around at the pictures on the wall; her daydream had made her nostalgic for her family members that were now gone. How much had happened to her since 1945! She wondered what her life would have been like had Danny and she kept their plans to move to Scotland after the war. Their lives had turned out very well, but much differently than they had planned during those first days of freedom.

Her thoughts drifted again to the book she had hoped to write about her time in Santo Tomas. Her story would not be complete without including the events that happened to Danny and her after the war. She settled back into her chair and let her mind wander back to the busy days when they first came to the United States...

We filled out the necessary government forms when we disembarked the "Lykes" and then were taken by the Red Cross to my parent's home. They lived in Highland Park, just a few miles northeast of Los Angeles. I remember how delighted the boys were to see the Arroyo Seco Highway—it seemed like such a marvel of engineering compared to the rudimentary streets we were accustomed to in Manila.

The reunion with my parents was blissful. Tommy, Lolita and Carol were also staying at the house, so we were able to share stories of our respective trips home from Manila. We weren't able to contain our emotions as we spent the day catching up on our time apart. My parents told us of their experiences on the East Coast when they first arrived in the U.S. They had moved to New York City, along with my brother Jack, and had enjoyed the lifestyle, if not the weather. Jack joined the Army in 1944 and was eventually stationed in southern California. When he wrote home extolling the virtues of Los Angeles, especially the glorious climate and beautiful surroundings, my parents immediately moved to California.

Danny and I told my parents of the horrifying experiences we had in Santo Tomas, particularly the difficult last year. Richard and Alan quickly made themselves at home and basked in the devotion of their grandparents. We were content for a couple of days to spend time talking, resting, and getting to know our new surroundings. When Danny was finally able to reach his managers at Ker and Co. he learned of the bleak economic conditions in Scotland. After much discussion, he made the decision to resign from the company and remain in Southern California.

My parent's house only had two bedrooms and two bathrooms and we had six adults and three children living there. It was obvious that Danny and I needed to strike out on our own. We possessed almost nothing; all of our possessions had either been confiscated by the Japanese or destroyed in the bombing of Manila. The only item we were allowed to bring with us from the Philippines was the camphor-wood chest that I had brought with me into camp.

None of us possessed suitable clothing. I had been issued a Woman's Army Corps uniform by the Red Cross and Danny was given a GI jacket. The boys had jackets made out of army blankets. The rest of our clothing was light and summery, inappropriate for the still-cool May weather in Highland Park. Parishioners at my parent's church gave me some used clothing of good quality, but because Danny was British they would not do the same for him. The British Consul had some second-hand clothing for him and in addition, lent him $400.

For a few days the question of money did not arise. The rumor of a payment of $2.90 per day for every day we had been interned turned out to be just that—a rumor. To further our frustration, I learned that my hasty resignation in December 1941 from my post at the High Commissioner's office had been very shortsighted: the U.S. government was providing three years of back pay to anyone who had been employed on January 1, 1942, when the Japanese entered Manila.

Danny was in no shape physically to return to work, but knew that we needed to move out of our cramped quarters quickly. He got a job in the accounting department of Chase and Sanborn Coffee Company just ten days after we arrived in Los Angeles. We were able to rent a tiny frame house in Highland Park within weeks. It was small, with just two bedrooms and one bath, but compared to the shanty it was a palace. Luckily the house was furnished so we could save our money for a home of our own. We lived contentedly in that house for five years.

Epilogue

Members of the Chapman and Watson family in 1946. From left, Thomas, Richard, Dora, Doreen, Alan and Kathleen.

Eventually we achieved a lifestyle similar to other young couples in the boom years of the 1950's. By the end of that era we were able to buy a beautiful home in Pasadena and two cars. Danny started his own accounting business. In 1950, once both boys were securely settled in school, I went to work and eventually joined Danny in the family business. We were both active in our community, volunteering our time and energy to Boy Scouts and the local police department. The boys joined sports teams, made close friends, and I am proud that they both achieved the rank of Eagle Scout.

Now as I think back on my life I dwell only on the happy times. I've lived a very contented life and, all things considered, a fortunate one.

Danny and Kathleen in their backyard on the occasion of their 60th wedding anniversary, June 20, 1996.

Afterword

The University of Santo Tomas remained as an internment camp until July, 1944. By that time, all of the internees who wished to repatriate to their home countries had departed. The few who remained in Santo Tomas were expatriates who had elected to stay in Manila but had no home to go to and no money with which to rent temporary quarters. In July, they were transferred to another camp and Santo Tomas began the slow conversion back to a school of higher education. The university quickly regained its prestigious reputation and today some of the Philippines' best and brightest students are among its alumni. Little of the campus looks the same as it did during those grim years when it served as an internment camp. There is a room in the Rector's Hall that is filled with memorabilia from the camp for those that wish to see artifacts left by the internees. A series of plaques adorns the entry hall in the Main building. The plaque commemorating the WWII years reads in part, "here Americans, British and other nationals were interned from January 1942 to February 1945. Here they were starved, dehumanized, left to die."

Thomas Chapman enjoyed his last years near his family and reveled in the visits from his children and grandchildren. He passed away from a heart attack in 1949 at the age of 76.

Dora Chapman volunteered in her community and at her church after Thomas' death. She babysat for her grandchildren and they remember her still for the cookies and cakes she baked for them. She died in 1962 of complications from a variety of illnesses.

Doreen Chapman joined the Navy WAVES after her return to the U.S. from the Philippines. She remained in the Navy, stationed in Northern California, until her death in 1968 from a heart attack at age 58.

Tommy Chapman continued his work with the U.S. Navy after his return to the U.S. He was a safety engineer at the Naval Ordinance Testing Station in China Lake, California, a remote location in the high desert of southern California. He, Lolita and their three children, Carol, Tom and Margaret, loved the beauty and serenity that is typical of the region. Tommy would descend into the crowded Los Angeles basin only for significant family occasions. He was a proficient fisherman and all-around outdoorsman and enjoyed an active life until his death from liver cancer in 1983 at the age of 71. Lolita continues to live in China Lake.

Jack Chapman always loved ham radio and electronics. After the war, Kathleen learned that Jack was one of the men who had smuggled in parts for the secret radio transmitter used in the camp. He was able to convert his love of audio work into a full-time career after the war. Jack went to work for a local radio station in Los Angeles, working with Bob Crane before his stint on "Hogan's Heroes". He was eventually recruited by the local CBS station in Los Angeles and worked for many years as the sound man for the "Two on the Town" program with Connie Chung. He retired in 1985 after heart problems required that he undergo bypass surgery. In 1987 he hosted a tour of Manila dubbed "Jack Chapman's Sentimental Journey" for 64 former internees. His affable personality and quick wit made the trip a huge success. Jack died in 1998 of heart failure at the age of 77.

Danny Watson worked in the family business he started until 1984. When he wasn't working, he indulged his love of fly fishing at the Pasadena Casting Club or puttered in his lush garden at home. For many years he served as the Volunteer Chief of Police in South Pasadena. He took many trips back to Scotland, returning every year once he retired. For many years he was the sole surviving member of his generation and consequently, he was adored and pampered by his numerous nephews and nieces who lived there. He never lost his love for Scotland and spoke constantly of moving back to his homeland someday. Danny died in 1997 of prostate cancer and complications from several strokes, just six months shy of his 90th birthday. He is missed by us all.

Kathleen Chapman Watson held a variety of jobs until her retirement in 1984. She was active in all of the boys' activities in school and found time to volunteer at the South Pasadena Library. In 1983 she returned to Manila for the first time since the war for her Central School reunion. She visited Santo Tomas, searching among the new buildings and patios for landmarks of the time she spent there. She recalls that the campus in 1983 was a far cry from her internee days, when it was a squalid scene filled with shanties. Today, she still plays bridge each week and is an active officer of the Pasadena Republican Women's Club. She takes special pride in her four grandchildren and two great-grandsons. The hallmark of her personality as a young woman—her infectious optimism—is still apparent today. She is adored by every member of the family.

Richard Watson graduated from high school in South Pasadena and has remained in his home town. He worked for Pacific Telephone as a young man and continued there until his retirement. Given his top-secret security clearance, he is still under contract to work on the telephone and data equipment needs at government installations. In 2002, he retired as a volunteer lieutenant with the South Pasadena Fire Department after a 40 year career. He is married to Marolyn and they have four children, Ann, Linda, Ricky and Brenda.

Alan Watson began a career in the commercial insurance business in California in 1964 and retired as a senior officer of his company in 1996. He has two children, Colin and Wendy. His two grandsons, Matthew and Jake, have provided him with unending depths of love and delight. In 1998, we relocated to Scottsdale, Arizona, where Alan plays golf twice a week—sometimes rather well. He is still cheeky.

Author's Note

Danny and Kathleen melted into society upon their return home, but as mainstream as they appeared, their Santo Tomas experience affected their outlook and attitude in many ways. Surviving three years in an internment camp enduring hunger, fear, and deprivation, provided them with a perspective that differed from their American friends. After the war, Danny and Kathleen never again took food, clothing or their liberty for granted.

Their internment sharpened their appreciation for the opportunities available to them, and spurred them on to attain great personal and professional success. They did not benefit from the G.I. Bill or receive any financial assistance from the government; they simply worked hard and met each challenge with unfailing optimism. They were proud that they had taken three years of nothing—no home, no food, no money, no freedom—and achieved the American dream.

Danny and Kathleen often discussed their time in Santo Tomas with friends, although they never allowed it to consume their lives. Kathleen has occasionally written the editor of the *Los Angeles Times,* responding to articles relating to prisoners of war, and she has been the featured speaker at civic functions, describing their years of internment. During many of her speaking engagements she has noticed that people frequently have a look of disappointment on their faces, and have said afterward that the Japanese prison camp experience seemed far less brutal than a Nazi concentration camp. Kathleen has surmised that these people are disappointed because they are looking for a more "exciting" story of torture and horror. She believes that there is no way to fully explain their experience to these people, but here is the response she provides them:

"No, we were not tortured in the conventional way one thinks of war-time torment. But there were degrees of pain and misery endured by the inhabitants of Santo Tomas that may be unfathomable to those who did not experience it firsthand. Families were torn apart, our homes and possessions confiscated and destroyed. We lived in crowded, noisy dormitories and rudimentary shanties. We were fed starvation rations and endured bouts with the diseases associated with such a meager diet. Those of us who were parents stood by helplessly as we watched our children suffer from malnutrition, crying from hunger, with no ability to provide food. And we lived our final year in captivity with the constant fear the Japanese military would treat us similarly to the residents of the other territories they captured."

When I first heard Kathleen relate this aspect of her speaking engagements I began to understand why so many people who survived horrendous wartime experiences returned home, never to talk about what they had faced. The magnitude of the pain and suffering cannot be quantified to those who were not there.

Danny and Kathleen were certainly not exceptional in their ability to endure their prison camp experience and go on to realize their dreams. During my research for this book I read many stories written by or about former internees of Santo Tomas. While each story is different and every prisoner's perspective was unique, one thread of consistency is woven through each account: the grit and determination that saw the prisoners through those horrible, dark days in the camp stayed with them through the remainder of their lives. As a group, they came back to their countries and achieved much.

Since the end of the war, some former internees have made efforts to obtain restitution from the Japanese government to compensate for their suffering, forfeited possessions, and loss of income. The Japanese have made no acknowledgement of these claims. Similarly, there have been overtures made to the United States Congress to compensate the American internees for the government's lack of protection and intervention after the bombing of Pearl Harbor. Again, no compensation has been offered. In 2001, the British government acknowledged that they had not provided adequate information and oversight to British citizens living in the Philippines, and gave each surviving internee 10,000 pounds.

There is really no way to fully acknowledge what the internees endured or to thank them for what they subsequently accomplished. But perhaps on those occasions when we remember the soldiers who served, we can also give our thanks and appreciation to the civilians who, in their own way, fought the good fight.

Bibliography

Bradley, James with Ron Powers, *Flags of Our Fathers,* New York: Bantam Books, 2000

Bradley, James, *Flyboys,* Boston, Little, Brown and Company, 2003

Cates, Tressa, *Infamous Santo Tomas,* San Marcos, CA: Pacific Press, 1981

Connaughton, Pimlott, Anderson, *The Battle for Manila,* Novato, CA: Presidio Press, 1995

Hartendorp, A.V.H., *The Santo Tomas Story,* New York: McGraw-Hill & Co., 1964

Holland, Robert, *The Rescue of Santo Tomas,* Paducah, KY., Turner Publishing, 2003

Lucas, Celia, *Prisoners of Santo Tomas,* London: Leo Cooper, Ltd., 1975

Manchester, William, *American Caesar,* Toronto: Little, Brown & Co., 1978

Nash, Grace, *That We Might Live,* Scottsdale, AZ: Shano Publishers, 1984

Sams, Margaret, *Forbidden Family,* Madison, WI: University of Wisconsin Press, 1989

Sides, Hampton, *Ghost Soldiers,* New York: Doubleday, 2001

Simpich, Frederick, "Return to Manila", *The National Geographic,* October, 1940

Stevens, Frederic, *Santo Tomas,* Stratford House, 1946

Sulzberger, C.L., *The American Heritage History of World War II,* American Heritage Publishing Company, 1966

Wetmore, Clio Matthews, *Beyond Pearl Harbor,* Haverford, PA: Infinity Publishing, 2001

Wygle, Peter, *Surviving a Japanese P.O.W. Camp,* Ventura, CA: Pathfinder Publishing, 1991

0-595-30877-5